DIE WALKÜRE

(THE WALKYR)

A MUSIC DRAMA IN THREE ACTS

FIRST PART OF THE TRILOGY

"DER RING DES NIBELUNGEN"

(THE NIBELUNG'S RING)

BY

RICHARD WAGNER

ENGLISH VERSION BY

CHARLES HENRY MELTZER

PUBLISHED BY

FRED. RULLMAN, INC., NEW YORK, N. Y.

THE WALKYR.

THE ARGUMENT.

ACT FIRST.

Siegmund, a warrior in flight, takes refuge one stormy evening in the house of Hunding, one of his enemies, whose wife, Sieglinde, arouses his interest and love. Hunding is bound by the laws of hospitality not to harm his guest till the morrow. In the night Sieglinde, having drugged her husband to sleep, elopes with the guest, who has plucked out a magic sword from a tree in which Wotan had plunged it. The lovers have, before this, discovered that they are twin brother and sister, children of Wotan in the form of a hero, Wälse.

ACT SECOND.

Fricka, the Goddess of Marriage, remonstrates with her truant husband, Wotan, on this outrage to her laws, and forces him to withdraw his favor from Siegmund and remove the power of his sword. A Walkyr (corpse-chooser), Brünnhilde, intended for his protection, is recalled and dispatched to tell him of his doom, but is so won upon by the hero's noble courage that she disobeys Wotan's command and strives to aid Siegmund in his combat with the pursuing Hunding. On this, Wotan intervenes in the fight himself, causing Siegmund's death. Then, killing the unoffending Hunding in his rage, he turns his anger against the Walkyr, who flies with Sieglinde.

ACT THIRD.

A band of Walkyrs is assembled on a mountain top, on the way to Walhalla with the bodies of chosen warriors. To them flies Brünnhilde for assistance, which they are disinclined to give. She resolves to save Sieglinde by sending her on, while she herself remains to bear the brunt of Wotan's anger. She tells Sieglinde that she shall be the mother of Siegfried, the greatest hero of the world, and that he shall restore the sword of which she gives her the pieces. Wotan furiously arrives, and, in spite of the intercession of the other Walkyrs, deprives Brünnhilde of her immortality and dooms her to lie in a charmed sleep for any man to wake and possess. All that he concedes to her pleadings is to place a protecting wall of fire around her, through which none but a hero may pass. Both know secretly that this deed is reserved for the unborn hero—Siegfried.

DRAMATIS PERSONÆ:

SIEGMUND	SIEGLINDE
HUNDING	BRÜNNHILDE
WOTAN	FRICKA

EIGHT WALKYRS.

DIE WALKÜRE.

Das Innere eines Wohnraumes.

In der Mitte steht der Stamm einer mächtigen Esche, dessen stark erhabene Wurzeln sich weithin in den Erdboden verlieren; von seinem Wipfel ist der Baum durch ein gezimmertes Dach geschieden, welches so durchschnitten ist, dass der Stamm und die nach allen Seiten hin sich ausstreckenden Aeste durch genau entsprechende Oeffnungen hindurch gehen; von dem belaubten Wipfel wird angenommen, dass er sich über dieses Dach ausbreite. Um den Eschenstamm, als Mittelpunkt, ist nun ein Saal gezimmert; die Wände sind aus roh behauenem Holzwerk, hie und da mit geflochtenen und gewebten Decken behangen. Rechts im Vordergrunde steht der Herd, dessen Rauchfang seitwärts zum Dache hinausführt; hinter dem Herde befindet sich ein innerer Raum, gleich einem Vorrathsspeicher, zu dem man auf einigen hölzernen Stufen hinaufsteigt; davor hängt, halb zurückgeschlagen, eine geflochtene Decke. Im Hintergrunde eine Eingangsthüre mit schlichtem Holzriegel. Links die Thüre zu einem inneren Gemache, zu dem gleichfalls Stufen hinaufführen; weiter vornen auf derselben Seite ein Tisch mit einer breiten, an der Wand angezimmerten Bank dahinter, und hölzernen Schemeln davor.

Ein kurzes Orchestervorspiel von heftiger, stürmischer Bewegung leitet ein. Wenn der Vorhang aufgeht, öffnet SIEGMUND von aussen hastig die Eingangsthür und tritt ein; es ist gegen Abend; starkes Gewitter, im Begriff, sich zu legen. — SIEGMUND hält einen Augenblick den Riegel in der Hand und überblickt den Wohnraum: er scheint von übermässiger Anstrengung erschöpft; sein Gewand und Aussehen zeigen, dass er sich auf der Flucht befinde. Da er Niemand gewahrt, schliesst er die Thür hinter sich, schreitet auf den Herd zu und wirft sich dort ermattet auf eine Decke von Bärenfell.

SIEGMUND.

Wess' Herd dies auch sei,
hier muss ich rasten.

(Er sinkt zurück und bleibt einige Zeit regungslos ausgestreckt, SIEGLINDE tritt aus der Thür des inneren Gemaches. Dem vernommenen Geräusche nach glaubte sie ihren Mann heimgekehrt: ihre ernste Miene zeigt sich dann verwundert, als sie einen Fremden am Herde ausgestreckt findet.)

SIEGLINDE
(noch im Hintergrunde).

Ein fremder Mann!
Ihn muss ich fragen.

(Sie tritt ruhig einige Schritte näher.)

Wer kam in's Haus
und liegt dort am Herd?

Da SIEGMUND sich nicht regt, tritt sie noch etwas näher und betrachtet ihn.)

Müde liegt er
von Weges Müh'n:
schwanden die Sinne ihm?
wäre er siech?

(Sie neigt sich näher zu ihm.)

Noch schwillt ihm der Athem;
das Auge nur schloss er; —
muthig dünkt mich der Mann,
sank er müd' auch hin.

SIEGMUND
(jäh das Haupt erhebend)

Ein Quell! ein Quell!

SIEGLINDE.

Erquickung schaff' ich.

(Sie nimmt schnell ein Trinkhorn, geht aus dem Haus und kommt mit dem gefüllten zurück, das sie SIEGMUND reicht.)

Labung biet' ich
dem lechzenden Gaumen:
Wasser, wie du gewollt!

(SIEGMUND trinkt und reicht ihr das Horn zurück. Nachdem er ihr mit dem Kopfe Dank zugewinkt, haftet sein Blick länger mit steigender Theilnahme an ihren Mienen.)

SIEGMUND.

Kühlende Labung
gab mir der Quell,
des Müden Last
machte er leicht;
erfrischt ist der Muth,
das Aug' erfreut
des Sehens selige Lust: —
wer ist's, der so mir es labt?

SIEGLINDE.

Dies Haus und dies Weib
sind Hundings Eigen;
gastlich gönn' er dir Rast:
harre bis heim er kehrt!

SIEGMUND

Waffenlos bin ich:
dem wunden Gast
wird dein Gatte nicht wehren.

SIEGLINDE
(besorgt).

Die Wunden weise mir schnell!

SIEGMUND
(schüttelt sich und springt lebhaft vom Lager zum Sitz auf).

Gering sind sie,
der Rede nicht werth;
noch fügen des Leibes
Glieder sich fest.
Hätten halb so stark wie mein Arm
Schild und Speer mir gehalten,
nimmer floh' ich dem Feind; —
doch zerschellten mir Speer und Schild.
Der Feinde Meute
hetzte mich müd',
Gewitter-Brunst
brach meinen Leib:

THE WALKYR.

The Interior of a Dwelling.

In the centre we behold the trunk of a mighty ash-tree, the far-spreading roots of which are gradually lost in the ground. The tree is separated from its crown by a timber-roof which is pierced, so that the trunk and all its branches pass through closely-fitting apertures; the thick-leafed crown is supposed to spread over this roof. A spacious hall is erected round this tree, which forms the centre; the walls consist of rough-hewn boards, hung here and there with plaited and woven covers. To the right, in the foreground, is the fire-place, the chimney of which passes out sideways through the roof. Behind the fire-place there is an inner space, resembling a store-room, which is reached by a few wooden steps, and separated from the fore-part of the hall by a plaited curtain half drawn back. In the background we perceive a door with a plain wooden bar. Another door to the left leads to an interior chamber which is also reached by steps. Further in the front, but on the same side, there is a table, and behind it a broad wooden bench fastened to the wall; a few wooden stools stand before the table.

The orchestra strikes up a brief prelude of a vehement character. As the curtain rises, SIEGMUND, approaching from without, opens the door hastily and enters. It is nearly evening; there has been a violent thunder storm, which is gradually passing away. SIEGMUND stops for a moment, and surveys the dwelling. He appears, exhausted and worn out with exertion. His looks and his disordered garments show him to be a fugitive. Finding no one in the room, he closes the door behind him, approaches the fire-place, and throws himself upon a bearskin rug.

SIEGMUND.

Whoe'er be my host,
Here will I slumber.

(He sinks back and remains stretched out motion-less for some time. SIEGLINDE enters through the door of the inner chamber. She has heard a noise which she believes to have been caused by the return of her husband, and she is not a little astonished at finding a stranger stretched out before the fireplace.)

SIEGLINDE.

(Still in the background.)
A stranger! See!
Him I must question.
(Advancing a few steps.)
Who came in here?
Who lies by yon hearth?
(As SIEGMUND does not stir, she approaches still nearer and looks at him attentively.)
Weary lies he,
With wand'ring worn.
Senseless, perchance, is he?
Can he be sick?
(Bending over him.)
Still breath in his body—
Though closed are his eye-lids.
Fearless he seems to me,
Though he fainting fell.

SIEGMUND.

(Suddenly lifting his head.)
A draught! A draught!

SIEGLINDE.

Relief I'll bring thee.
(She gets a drinking-horn quickly, leaves the house, but comes back soon after filling the vessel with water, which she hands to SIEGMUND.)
Drink and moisten
Thy lips that now languish.
Water, as thou hast wished!
(SIEGMUND drinks and returns the horn. After nodding his thanks to her, he regards her with increasing attention.)

SIEGMUND.

Cooling and comfort
Came from the well;
My weight of woe
Lighter it made.
Refreshed is my heart,
Again my eyes
With gladness gaze on the world.
Who was't that brought me relief?

SIEGLINDE.

This house and myself
Belong to Hunding;
Shelter ne'er he'd deny.
Tarry till home he comes.

SIEGMUND.

Weaponless, wounded—
A guest so weak
Will be safe with thy husband.

SIEGLINDE.

(Alarmed.)
Thou'rt wounded? Show me thy wounds?

SIEGMUND.

(Shaking himself, springing up quickly, and sitting down.)
They're trifles, all;
They call not for care.
The limbs of my body
All are still whole.
Had my shield and spear been as strong,
Half as strong as my arm was,
Ne'er the foe I had fled.
But now broken are spear and shield.
My foes were many—
Pressed me too hard;
The furious storm
Wore out my strength.

doch schneller als ich der Meute,
schwand die Müdigkeit mir:
sank auf die Lider mir Nacht,
die Sonne lacht mir nun neu.

SIEGLINDE
(hat ein Horn mit Meth gefüllt und reicht es ihm).

Des seimigen Methes
süssen Trank
mög'st du mir nicht verschmäh'n.

SIEGMUND.

Schmecktest du mir ihn zu?

(SIEGLINDE nippt am Horne und reicht es ihm
wieder; Siegmund thut einen langen Zug; dann setzt
er schnell ab und reicht das Horn zurück. Beide
blicken sich, mit wachsender Ergriffenheit, eine Zeit
lang stumm an.)

SIEGMUND
(mit bebender Stimme).

Einen Unseligen labtest du: —
Unheil wende
der Wunsch von dir!

(Er bricht schnell auf, um fortzugehen.)

Gerastet hab' ich
und süss geruh't:
weiter wend' ich den Schritt.

SIEGLINDE
(lebhaft sich umwendend).

Wer verfolgt dich, dass du schon flieh'st?

SIEGMUND
(von ihrem Rufe gefesselt, wendet sich wieder: langsam und düster).

Misswende folgt mir,
wohin ich fliehe;
Misswende naht mir,
wo ich mich neige:
dir Frau doch bleibe sie fern!
Fort wend' ich Fuss und Blick.

(Er schreitet schnell zur Thür und hebt den Riegel.)

SIEGLINDE
(in heftigem Selbstvergessen ihm nachrufend).

So bleibe hier!
Nicht bringst du Unheil dahin,
Wo Unheil im Hause wohnt!

SIEGMUND
(bleibt tief erschüttert stehen und forscht in SIEG-
LINDE'S Mienen; diese schlägt endlich verschämt
und traurig die Augen nieder. Langes Schweigen.
SIEGMUND kehrt zurück und lässt sich, an den Herd
gelehnt, nieder).

Wehwalt hiess ich mich selbst: —
Hunding will ich erwarten.

(SIEGLINDE verharrt in betretenem Schweigen; dann
fährt sie auf, lauscht und hört HUNDING, der sein
Ross aussen zu Stall führt; sie geht hastig zur Thüre
und öffnet.)

(HUNDING, gewaffnet mit Schild und Speer, tritt
ein, und hält unter der Thür, als er SIEGMUND
gewahrt.)

SIEGLINDE
(dem ernst fragenden Blicke, den HUNDING auf sie
richtet, entgegnend).

Müd' am Herd
Fand ich den Mann:
Noth führt' ihn in's Haus.

HUNDING.

Du labtest ihn?

SIEGLINDE.

Den Gaumen letzt' ich ihm,
Gastlich sorgt' ich sein'.

SIEGMUND
(der HUNDING fest und ruhig beobachtet)

Dach und Trank
Dank ich ihr:
Willst du dein Weib drum schelten?

HUNDING.

Heilig ist mein Herd: —
Heilig sei dir mein Haus!

(Zu SIEGLINDE, indem er die Waffen ablegt un
ihr übergibt).

Rüst' uns Männern das Mahl!

(SIEGLINDE hängt die Waffen am Eschenstamm
auf, holt Speise und Trank aus dem Speicher un
rüstet auf dem Tische das Nachtmahl.)

HUNDING.
(misst scharf und verwundert SIEGMUND'S Züge
die er mit denen seiner Frau vergleicht; für sich)

Wie gleicht er dem Weibe!
Der gleisende Wurm
glänzt auch ihm aus dem Auge.

(Er birgt sein Befremden und wendet sich unbefange
an SIEGMUND).

Weit her, traun!
kamst du des Weg's;
ein Ross nicht ritt,
der Rast hier fand:
welch' schlimme Pfade
schufen dir Pein?

SIEGMUND.

Durch Wald und Wiese,
Haide und Hain,
jagte mich Sturm
und starke Noth:
nicht kenn' ich den Weg, den ich kam
Wohin ich irrte,
weiss ich noch minder:
Kunde gewänn' ich dess' gern.

HUNDING
(am Tische und SIEGMUND den Sitz bietend).

Dess' Dach dich deckt,
Dess' Haus dich hegt,
Hunding heisst der Wirth;
wendest von hier du
nach West den Schritt,
In Höfen reich
hausen dort Sippen,
die Hunding's Ehre behüten.
Gönnt mir Ehre mein Gast,
wird sein Name nun mir genannt.

(SIEGMUND, der sich am Tisch niedergesetzt
blickt nachdenklich vor sich hin. SIEGLINDE ha
sich neben HUNDING, SIEGMUND gegenüber, ge
setzt und heftet mit auffallender Theilnahme und
Spannung ihr Auge auf diesen.)

HUNDING
(der beide beobachtet).

Trägst du Sorge,
mir zu vertrau'n,
der Frau hier gieb doch Kunde,
sieh', wie gierig sie dich frägt!

ut fast did I flee the hunters;
aster still I grew strong.
Night at last darkened my eyes;
he sun now cheers me anew.

SIEGLINDE.
(Filling a horn with mead and handing it to him.)

Thou wilt not deny me—
Here is mead.
Sweet is the cloying drink.

SIEGMUND.

Wilt thou not taste it first?
(SIEGLINDE sips a little, and hands him the horn again.
SIEGMUND takes a long draught; then stopping suddenly, he returns the horn. For a long time the two
remain silent, looking at each other with growing
interest.)

SIEGMUND.
(With trembling voice.)

Thou hast cheered one to misfortune
doomed.
May no evil
Reward thy care!
(He rises hastily, as if about to leave.)

I've rested—fully
Restored I feel.
Now I'll wend on my way.

SIEGLINDE.
(Turning round quickly.)

Who pursues thee? Why must thou go?

SIEGMUND.
(Stopping at her call; slowly and gloomily.)

Mischief pursues me,
Where'er I wander;
Mischief attends me—
Ne'er can I flee it.
But thee Fate surely shall spare.
Far from thy path I'll fly!
(Approaching the door, he lifts the bar.)

SIEGLINDE.
(Calling him back in utter self-abnegation.)

Ah, do but stay!
What curse canst thou bring to one
Who dwells in a house accurst?

SIEGMUND.
(Lingers deeply moved, trying to read the eyes of
SIEGLINDE, who stands abashed and embarrassed. A
long silence follows. SIEGMUND returns, and resumes
his seat by the hearth.)

"Woeful" named I myself:—
Hunding I will await here.
(SIEGLINDE remains silent and embarrassed. Suddenly
she starts up, listens, and hears HUNDING, who leads
his steed to the stable. She hastens to open the door.)

———

(Enter HUNDING, armed with shield and spear. In
the doorway he stops on beholding SIEGMUND.)

SIEGLINDE.
(Meeting the questioning look of HUNDING.)

Weak and worn
Found I this man:
Need drove him our way.

HUNDING.

Thou'st tended him?

SIEGLINDE.

His thirsting lips I cooled;
Gave our guest good cheer.

SIEGMUND.
(Viewing HUNDING firmly and calmly.)

Rest and drink,
Did she give.
Would'st thou rebuke her bounty?

HUNDING.

Sacred is my hearth—
Safe art thou in my house!
(To SIEGLINDE, giving her his weapons.)

Bring us men-folk our meal!
(SIEGLINDE hangs the weapons on the trunk of the
tree, fetches meat and drink from the larder
and prepares the meal on the table.)

HUNDING.
(Scanning SIEGMUND's features sharply and comparing
them with his wife's. Aside:)

How like her he seemeth!
The same wicked gleam
Comes and goes in his glances.
(Concealing his surprise and turning to SIEGMUND.)

Far, forsooth,
Must thou have come.
No horse had he
Who here found rest.
What dreadful doings
Brought thee thy pain?

SIEGMUND.

Through wood and meadow,
Forest and heath,
Trouble and storm
Beset my course.
Naught know I of how here I came.
And where I wandered
Know I no better.
Fain would I learn who's my host!

HUNDING.
(Seating himself at the table and beckoning SIEGMUND
to a seat.)

This shelt'ring roof,
This friendly house,
Both are Hunding's own.
Shouldst thou bend westward
Thy steps from hence,
In manors rich
Kinsmen will greet thee,
Who guard the honor of Hunding.
Glad were I if my guest
Would his name to me now make known.
(SIEGMUND, sitting at the table, remains silent. SIEG-
LINDE, seated by the side of HUNDING, and opposite
SIEGMUND, observes the latter with undisguised sym-
pathy and attention.)

HUNDING.
(Watching them both.)

Shouldst thou shrink from
Trusting thy host,
Thy hostess here will listen;
See, she hangs upon thy words!

SIEGLINDE
(unbefangen und theilnahmvoll).
Gast, wer du bist,
wüsst' ich gern.

SIEGMUND
(blickt auf, sieht ihr in das Auge und beginnt ernst).
Friedmund darf ich nicht heissen;
Frohwalt möcht' ich wohl sein:
doch Wehwalt muss ich mich nennen.
Wolfe, der war mein Vater;
zu zwei kam ich zur Welt,
eine Zwillingsschwester und ich.
Früh schwanden mir
Mutter und Maid;
die mich gebar,
und die mit mir sie barg,
kaum hab' ich sie je gekannt. —
Wehrlich und stark war Wolfe;
Der Feinde wuchsen ihm viel.
Zum Jagen zog
mit dem Jungen der Alte;
von Hetze und Harst
einst kehrten wir heim:
da lag das Wolfsnest leer;
zu Schutt gebrannt
der prangende Saal,
zum Stumpf der Eiche
blühender Stamm;
erschlagen der Mutter
muthiger Leib,
verschwunden in Gluthen
der Schwester Spur:
uns schuf die herbe Noth
der Neidinge harte Schaar.
Geächtet floh
der Alte mit mir;
lange Jahre
lebte der Junge
mit Wolfe im wilden Wald:
manche Jagd
ward auf sie gemacht;
doch muthig wehrte
das Wolfspaar sich.
(Zu HUNDING gewendet.)
Ein Wölfing kündet dir das,
den als Wölfing mancher wohl kennt.

HUNDING.
Wunder und wilde Märe
kündest du, kühner Gast,
Wehwalt — der Wölfing!
Mich dünkt, von dem wehrlichen Paar
vernahm ich dunkle Sage,
Kannt' ich auch Wolfe
und Wölfing nicht.

SIEGLINDE.
Doch weiter künde, Fremder,
wo weilt dein Vater jetzt?

SIEGMUND.
Ein starkes Jagen auf uns
stellten die Neidinge an:
der Jäger viele
fielen den Wölfen,
in Flucht durch den Wald
trieb sie das Wild:
wie Spreu zerstob' uns der Feind.
Doch ward ich vom Vater versprengt:
seine Spur verlor ich,
je länger ich forschte;
nur traf ich im Forst:
leer lag das vor mir,
den Vater fand ich nicht. —
Aus dem Wald trieb es mich fort;
mich drängt' es zu Männern und Frauen
wie viel ich traf,
wo ich sie fand,
eines Wolfes Fell
ob ich um Freund,
um Frauen warb, —
immer doch war ich geächtet,
Unheil lag auf mir.
Was rechtes je ich rieth,
andern dünkte es arg;
was schlimm immer mir schien,
andre gaben ihm Gunst.
In Fehde fiel ich,
wo ich mich fand;
Zorn traf mich,
wohin ich zog;
gehrt' ich nach Wonne,
weckt' ich nur Weh': —
drum musst' ich mich Wehwalt nennen,
des Wehes waltet' ich nur.

HUNDING.
Die so leidig Loos dir beschied,
nicht liebte dich die Norn:
froh nicht grüsst dich der Mann,
dem fremd als Gast du nah'st.

SIEGLINDE.
Feige nur fürchten den,
der waffenlos einsam fährt! —
Künde noch, Gast,
wo du im Kampf
zuletzt die Waffe verlor'st!

SIEGMUND
(immer lebhafter).
Ein trauriges Kind
rief mich zum Trutz:
vermählen wollte
der Magen Sippe
dem Mann ohne Minne die Maid.
Wider den Zwang
zog ich zum Schutz;
der Dränger Tross
traf ich im Kampf:

SIEGLINDE.
(With artless curiosity.)
Fain would I know,
Friend, thy name.

SIEGMUND.
(Looking up, catches her eager glances, and answers seriously:)
"Peaceful" no one may name me;
"Joyful" fain I would be.
But "Woeful," that were more fitting.
Wolfè, he was my father;
And one am I of twins—
With a sister saw I the light.
    Soon went from me
    Mother and maid;
    She who was born,
    And she who gave us birth.
Hardly my dear ones I'd known.
Stalwart and strong was Wolfè;
But foes a-many had he.
    The father fared
    To a hunt with the stripling;
    With baiting worn out,
    Their home they regained.
They found their lair laid waste!
    The stately hall
    In ruins now lay—
    The oak once mighty
    Dwarfed to a stump.
    And stark lay the mother,
    Wantonly slain—
    All trace of the sister
    By flame devoured.
Weighed down by bitter want,
By envious hosts hemmed round,
    An outcast now,
    ⸙ fled wit my sire.
Years and years then
Wandered the stripling
With Wolfè amid the woods.
Many packs
Pressed hard on their trail,
But bravely ever
The wolves stood fast.
    (Turning to HUNDING.)
A wolf-cub tells thee this tale,
Who a wolf to many has seemed.

HUNDING.
Wonders and wild, weird stories
Tellest thou, hardy guest.
"Woeful"—the wolf-cub!
Methinks I had heard the grim tale
That round ye twain is woven.
    Known to me's neither
    This wolf nor cub.

SIEGLINDE.
But tell me more, O stranger,
Where dwells thy father now?

SIEGMUND.
Our foes pressed hard on our heels,
Hunted us hotly and fast.
    And many hunters
    Fell, as the quarry,
    In flight through the woods,
    Swept them away.
Like chaff we scattered the foe.
At last, though, my father I lost—
    Ev'ry trace had vanished,
    Though steadfast I sought him.
    But a wolf-skin found I
    Deep in a glade.
    Void now was the world—
    My father gone for aye!
Then the woods had no more joy:
I hungered for men-folk and women.
    And men I met,
    And women found,
    But whether friend
    Or love I sought,
Still I was held as an outcast;
Evil dogged my path.
Though right might be my rede,
Others held it as ill.
What ill seemed in my eyes
Others took to be good.
    In feuds entangled,
    On every side;
    Wrath met me
    Go where I would.
    Thirsting for pleasure,
    Sorrow I found;
So now they could "Woeful" name me,
For woe had marked all my way.

HUNDING.
Since so hard thy lot has been made,
By Fate thou'st not been spoilt;
Warmly greets thee no man
Whose guest thou hap'st to be.

SIEGLINDE.
Dastards may dread him
Who weaponless goes his way.
    Tell us, O guest,
    Where—in what fight—
Thy sword was wrung from thy hand

SIEGMUND.
(More animated.)
    A maiden forlorn
    Called for my aid:
    Perforce her kinsmen
    Had wished her wedded—
The maid to a lover unloved.
    Hasting to help
    Swung I my sword;
    The tyrant's train
    Met but to rout—

dem Sieger sank der Feind.
Erschlagen lagen die Brüder:
die Leichen umschlang da die Maid;
den Grimm verjagt' ihr der Gram.
Mit wilder Thränen Fluth
betroff sie weinend die Wal:
um des Mordes der eig'nen Brüder
klagte die unsel'ge Braut. —

    Der Erschlag'nen Sippen
    stürmten daher;
    übermächtig
    ächzten nach Rache sie,
    rings um die Stätte
    ragten mir Feinde.
    Doch von der Wal
    wich nicht die Maid:
    mit Speer und Schild
    schirmt' ich sie lang',
    bis Speer und Schild
    im Harst mir zerhau'n.
Wund und waffenlos stand ich —
sterben sah ich die Maid:
mich hetzte das wüthende Heer —
auf den Leichen lag sie todt.
(Mit einem Blicke voll schmerzlichen Feuers auf
SIEGLINDE.)
Nun weisst du, fragende Frau,
Warum ich — Friedmund nicht heisse!
(Er steht auf und schreitet an den Herd zu. SIEG-
LINDE blickt erbleichend und tief erschüttert zu
Boden.)

HUNDING
(sehr finster).

Ich weiss ein wildes Geschlecht,
    nicht heilig ist ihm,
    was Andern hehr:
verhasst ist es Allen und mir.
Zur Rache ward ich gerufen,
    Sühne zu nehmen
    Für Sippen-Blut:
    zu spät kam ich
    und kehrte nun heim,
des flücht'gen Frevlers Spur
im eig'nen Haus zu erspäh'n. —
    Mein Haus hütet,
    Wölfing, dich heut':
für die Nacht nahm ich dich auf:
    mit starker Waffe
    doch wehre dich morgen;
zum Kampfe kies' ich den Tag:
für Todte zahlst du mir Zoll.
(Zu SIEGLINDE, die sich mit besorgter Geberde
zwischen die beiden Männer stellt.)
    Fort aus dem Saal!
    Säume hier nicht!
Den Nachttrunk rüste mir d'rin,
und harre mein' zur Ruh'.

(SIEGLINDE nimmt sinnend ein Trinkhorn vom
Tisch, geht zu einem Schrein, aus dem sie Würze
nimmt, und wendet sich nach dem Seitengemache:
auf der obersten Stufe bei der Thüre angelangt, wendet sie sich noch einmal um und richtet auf SIEG-
MUND — der mit verhaltenem Grimme ruhig am
Herde steht und einzig sie im Auge behält — einen
langen, sehnsüchtigen Blick, mit welchem sie ihn
endlich auf eine Stelle im Eschenstamme bedeutungs-
voll auffordernd hinweist. HUNDING, der ihr Zögern
bemerkt, treibt sie dann mit einem gebietenden Winke
fort, worauf sie mit dem Trinkhorn und der Leuchte
durch die Thüre verschwindet.)

HUNDING
(nimmt seine Waffen vom Baume).

Mit Waffen wehrt sich der Mann. —
Dich Wölfing, treffe ich morgen:
    mein Wort hörtest du —
    hüte dich wohl!
(Er geht mit den Waffen in das Gemach ab.)

SIEGMUND
(allein).

(Es ist vollständig Nacht geworden; der Saal ist nur
noch von einem matten Feuer im Herde erhellt
SIEGMUND lässt sich, nah beim Feuer, auf das Lager nieder, und brütet in grosser Aufregung eine Zeit
lang schweigend vor sich hin.)

Ein Schwert verhiess mir der Vater,
ich fänd' es in höchster Noth. —
    Waffenlos fiel ich
    in Feindes Haus:
    seiner Rache Pfand
    raste ich hier: —
    ein Weib sah' ich,
    wonnig und hehr;
    entzückend Bangen
    zehrt mein Herz: —
zu der mich nun Sehnsucht zieht,
die mit süssem Zauber mich sehrt —
im Zwange hält sie der Mann,
der mich — Wehrlosen höhnt. —
    Wälse! Wälse!
    Wo ist dein Schwert?
    Das starke Schwert,
    das im Sturm ich schwänge,
Bricht mir hervor aus der Brust,
was wüthend das Herz noch hegt?
(Das Feuer bricht zusammen; es fällt aus der auf-
sprühenden Gluth ein greller Schein auf die Stelle
des Eschenstammes, welche Sieglinde's Blick bezeich-
net hatte und an der man jetzt deutlicher einen
Schwertgriff haften sieht.)
    Was gleiszt dort hell
    im Glimmerschein?
    Welch' ein Strahl bricht
    aus der Esche Stamm? —
    Des Blinden Auge
    leuchtet ein Blitz:
lustig lacht da der Blick. —
    Wie der Schein so hehr
    das Herz mir sengt!
    Ist es der Blick
    der blühenden Frau,
    den dort haftend
    sie hinter sich liess,
als aus dem Saal sie schied?
(Von hier an verglimmt das Herdfeuer allmälig.)
    Nächtiges Dunkel
    deckte mein Aug',
    ihres Blickes Strahl
    streifte mich da:
Wärme gewann ich und Tag.

A victor trod the field.
All stark in death lay the brothers;
The maid to their corses still clung,
In horror deeper than hate.
With floods of rushing tears
She mourned and moaned for her dead—
For the loss of her slaughtered brothers,
Wept the most wretched of brides.
 Then the dead ones' kinsmen
 Burst on the scene,
 Overwhelming,
 Thirsting for vengeance dire;
 Foemen ringed round me,
 Pressing me harder.
 Still to her dead
 Close clung the maid.
 With shield and spear
 Stood I, her screen,
 Till spear and shield
 Were hewn from my hand.
Wounded—weaponless stood I—
Saw the maid as she fell.
I fled from the merciless host—
On the corses...she lay dead.

(Looking sorrowfully at SIEGLINDE.)

Thou'st heard now what thou wouldst
 know,
Why no one "Peaceful" may name me!

[He rises and walks to the hearth. SIEGLINDE, much moved, looks down.)

HUNDING.
(Gloomily.)

A brood I know that's accurst,
 Naught holy it holds
 Where others bow:
 'Tis hated of all and of me.
To right a wrong I was chosen,
 Vengeance to render
 For kinsmen slain.
 Too late came I,
 But now I return
The fleeing murd'rer's trace
To find at last in my home.
 My roof shields thee,
 Wolf-cub, to-night:
Until morn be thou my guest.
 But 'ware the morrow,
 And look to thy weapons.
Full soon I'll meet thee in arms—
For blood shed, blood thou shalt pay!

(To SIEGLINDE, who has anxiously moved between the two men.)

 Hence from the hall!
 Tarry not here!
My night-draught brew in yon room:
 Await me there, within!

(SIEGLINDE takes pensively a drinking-horn from the table, walks to a cupboard from which she takes spices, and goes to the chamber. On reaching the uppermost step near the door, she turns her head toward SIEG-MUND, who stands calmly and sullenly by the fire-place, never losing sight of her. She casts a long and signifi-

cant glance at him, by which she endeavors to direct his attention to a certain spot in the ash-tree. HUNDING notices her strange hesitation, and warns her away with a commanding look, whereupon she disappears through the door with the torch and drinking-horn.)

HUNDING.
(Takes his weapons off the tree.)

With weapons should men keep ward.
To-morrow, Wolf-cub, I'll meet thee!
 My words thou hast heard—
 Guard thyself well!

(He goes into the adjoining room, taking his weapons with him.)

SIEGMUND.
(Alone.)

(Night has now fallen. The hall is dimly lighted by the dying fire. SIEGMUND lies down on the couch by the hearth, and remains brooding and silent for some time, much agitated.)

A sword—so promised my father—
I'd find in my hour of need.
 Weaponless am I,
 My host a foe.
 By his wrath fore-doomed,
 Here I now lie.
 A woman came,
 Witching and pure;
 And ravishing anguish
 Burns my heart;
But she for whom I now long,
Who has cast about me her spell,
Is held in thrall by the man
Who scorns—me, all unarmed.—
 Wälse! Wälse!
 Where is thy sword?
 The strong, good sword
 That in fight went flashing!
Burst from my sorrowful breast
The frenzy my heart had hid!

(The smoldering cinders on the hearth fall to pieces; a clear light from the resulting glow shines on the tree, illuminating the spot which SIEGLINDE's glance had designated, and reveals the handle of a sword.)

 What glistens there?
 What flames and gleams?
 See—a light streams
 From the ashen stem:
 So bright it dazzles
 Eyes that were blind—
Laughs with light at my look!
 In the glorious glow
 My heart takes fire!
 Is it the glance
 That woman so fair
 Left behind her
 To burn in the tree,
When from the hall she stole?

(From now on the fire on the hearth begins to die out.)

 Night and its darkness
 Hung on my lids:
 But her beaming eyes
 Gladdened my gloom,
Warmed me and won back the light.

Selig schien mir
der Sonne Licht,
den Scheitel umgliss mir
ihr wonniger Glanz —
bis hinter Bergen sie sank.
Noch einmal, da sie schied,
traf mich Abends ihr Schein;
selbst der alten Esche Stamm
erglänzte in gold'ner Gluth:
da bleicht die Blüthe —
das Licht verlischt —
nächt'ges Dunkel
deckt mir das Auge:
tief in des Busens Berge
glimmt nur noch lichtlose Gluth!

(Das Feuer ist gänzlich verloschen; volle Nacht. —
Das Seitengemach öffnet sich leise: SIEGLINDE, in
weissem Gewande, tritt heraus und schreitet auf
SIEGMUND zu.)

SIEGLINDE.

Schläfst du, Gast?

SIEGMUND
(freudig überrascht aufspringend).

Wer schleicht daher?

SIEGLINDE
(mit geheimnissvoller Hast).

Ich bin's, höre mich an! —
In tiefem Schlaf liegt Hunding;
ich würzt' ihm betäubenden Trank.
Nütze die Nacht dir zum Heil!

SIEGMUND
(hitzig unterbrechend).

Heil macht mich dein Nah'n!

SIEGLINDE.

Eine Waffe lass' mich dir weisen —
O merke wohl, was ich dir melde! —
Den hehrsten Helden
dürft' ich dich heissen;
dem Stärksten allein
ward sie bestimmt.
O merke wohl, was ich dir melde! —
Der Männer Sippe
sass hier im Saal,
von Hunding zur Hochzeit geladen:
er freite ein Weib,
das ungefragt
Schächer ihm schenkten zur Frau.
Traurig sass ich,
während sie tranken:
ein Fremder trat da herein —
ein Greis in grauem Gewand;
tief hing ihm der Hut,
der deckt' ihm der Augen eines;
doch des andren Strahl,
Angst schuf er allen,
traf die Männer
sein mächt'ges Dräu'n:
mir allein
weckte das Auge
süss sehnenden Harm,

Thränen und Trost zugleich.
Auf mich blickt' er
und blitzte auf Jene,
als ein Schwert in Händen er schwang
das stiess er nun
in der Esche Stamm,
bis zum Heft haftet' es drin: —
dem sollte der Stahl geziemen,
der aus dem Stamm' es zög'.
Der Männer Alle,
so kühn sie sich müh'ten,
die Wehr sich keiner gewann:
Gäste kamen,
und Gäste gingen,
die stärksten zogen am Stahl —
keinen Zoll entwich er dem Stamm:
dort haftet schweigend das Schwert. —
Da wusst' ich, wer der war,
der mich Gramvolle gegrüsst:
ich weiss auch,
wem allein
im Stamm das Schwert er bestimmt.
O fänd' ich ihn heut'
und hier, den Freund;
käm' er aus Fremden
zur ärmsten Frau:
was je ich gelitten
in grimmigem Leid,
was je mich geschmerzt
in Schande und Schmach, —
süsseste Rache
sühnte dann Alles!
Erjagt hätt' ich,
was je ich verlor;
was je ich beweint,
wär' mir gewonnen —
fänd 'ich den heiligen Freund,
umfing' den Helden mein Arm!

SIEGMUND
(umfasst sie mit feuriger Gluth).

Dich, selige Frau,
hält nun der Freund,
dem Waffe und Weib bestimmt!
Heiss in der Brust
brennt mir der Eid,
der mich dir Edlen vermählt.
Was je ich ersehnt,
ersah ich in dir;
in dir fand ich,
was je mir gefehlt!
Littest du Schmach,
und schmerzte mich Leid;
war ich geächtet,
und warst du entehrt;
freudige Rache
lacht nun den Frohen!
Auf lach' ich
in heiliger Lust,

Sweet the sunshine
Now seems to me.
Its ravishing radiance
Enwrapped me around—
Till 'mid the mountains it died.
And once more, ere it went,
Came to-night the glad gleam,
And the old, old ashen stem,
Grew brighter and gleamed as gold.
The flush has faded—
The light grows dim—
Night and darkness
Weigh on my eyelids.
Deep in my bosom only
Gleameth in secret a flame.

(The fire is now quite out. It is deep night. The chamber door opens softly. SIEGLINDE, clad in white, enters and draws near to SIEGMUND.)

SIEGLINDE.

Sleep'st thou, guest?

SIEGMUND.

(Springing up in joyful surprise.)
Who steals this way?

SIEGLINDE.

(Mysteriously and in haste.)
Hear me, friend; it is I!
Opprest with sleep lies Hunding;
I seasoned his draught with a drug.
Use thou the night for thy weal!

SIEGMUND.

(Interrupting her eagerly.)
Bliss comes now thou'rt near!

SIEGLINDE.

But a weapon first I would show thee—
O would that thou couldst win't!
The highest hero
Then could I call thee—
The mightiest alone
Owns it as lord!
O pay good heed now to my story!
The host of kinsmen
Sat in the hall,
By Hunding bid here to a wedding.
A woman he wooed
Whom all by force,
Robbers had brought him for bride.
Sadly sat I
While they were drinking:
A stranger slowly strode in—
An agèd man, all in grey.
Pressed low on his head,
One eye had his hat kept hidden;
But the other flamed,
Awful and boding,
All it threatened
On whom it gazed.
I alone
Shrank not in terror,
Felt sad and yet glad,

Tearful and hopeful both!
On me looked he,
And flared at the others;
Then a sword uplifted he swung,
And drove it deep
In the ashen stem—
To the hilt hewed it a way.
He who from the tree could draw it
Should some day own the steel.
The men sought vainly,
They strove and they struggled,
The wondrous weapon to win:—
Guests a-coming,
And guests a-going,
The strongest tugged at the steel—
Not an inch it budged from the stem.
There buried still lies the sword.
Well knew I who was he
That had greeted me who grieved.
I know, too,
Who alone
The sword is destined to win.
O would he were here,
And now, that friend!
Come from a far land
To give me aid.
Whate'er I have suffered
Of bitterest pain—
Whate'er was my load
Of scorn and of shame,
Sweetest of vengeance
Comfort should bring me.
Regained were all
That I e'er had lost;
Whate'er I had mourned
Would be recovered;
Could I but find him, that friend—
And press my lord to my breast!

SIEGMUND.

(Embracing her ardently.)
Then here in his arms
Holds thee that friend,
Who weapon and wife should win!
Hot from my heart
Take now the oath
That weds me, dearest, to thee.
Whate'er I had dreamt
In thee I divined;
In thee found all
That e'er I had craved!
Shame thou hast known,
And pain have I borne;
Outcast I've wandered,
Dishonored thou'st been.
Now at last vengeance
Comes to delight us!
Loud laugh I
In holiest joy —

halt' ich dich Hehre umfangen,
fühl' ich dein schlagendes Herz!

SIEGLINDE
(fährt erschrocken zusammen und reisst sich los).

Ha, wer ging? wer kam herein?

(Die hintere Thüre ist aufgesprungen und bleibt weit
geöffnet: aussen herrliche Frühlingsnacht; der Voll-
mond leuchtet herein und wirft sein helles Licht auf
das Paar, das so sich plötzlich in voller Deutlichkeit
wahrnehmen kann.)

SIEGMUND
(in leiser Entzückung).

Keiner ging —
doch Einer kam:
siehe, der Lenz
lacht in den Saal!

(Er zieht sie mit sanftem Ungestüm zu sich auf das
Lager.)

Winterstürme wichen
dem Wonnemond,
in mildem Lichte
leuchtet der Lenz;
auf linden Lüften,
leicht und lieblich,
Wunder webend
er sich wiegt;
über Wald und Auen
weht sein Athem,
weit geöffnet
lacht sein Aug'.
Aus sel'ger Vöglein Sange
süss er tönt,
holde Düfte
haucht er aus;
seinem warmen Blut entblühen
wonnige Blumen,
Keim und Spross
entspriesst seiner Kraft.
Mit zarter Waffen Zier
bezwingt er die Welt.
Winter und Sturm wichen
der starken Wehr: —
wohl musste den tapfern Streichen
die strenge Thüre auch weichen,
die trotzig und starr
uns — trennte von ihm. —
Zu seiner Schwester
schwang er sich her;
die Liebe lockte den Lenz;
in uns'rem Busen
barg sie sich tief:
nun lacht sie selig dem Licht.
Die bräutliche Schwester
befreite der Bruder;
zertrümmert liegt,
was je sie getrennt;
jauchzend grüsst sich
das junge Paar:
vereint sind Liebe und Lenz!

SIEGLINDE.

Du bist der Lenz,

nach dem ich verlangte
in frostigen Winter's Frist:
dich grüsste mein Herz
mit heiligem Grau'n,
als dein Blick zuerst mir erblühte. —
Fremdes nur sah ich von je,
freundlos war mir das Nahe;
als hätt' ich nie es gekannt
war was immer mir kam.
Doch dich kannt' ich
deutlich und klar:
Als mein Auge dich sah,
warst du mein Eigen:
was im Busen ich barg,
was ich bin,
hell wie der Tag
taucht' es mir auf,
wie tönender Schall
schlug's an mein Ohr,
als in frostig öder Fremde
zuerst ich den Freund ersah.

(Sie hängt sich entzückt an seinen Hals und blickt
ihm nahe in's Gesicht.)

SIEGMUND.

O süsseste Wonne!
Seligstes Weib!

SIEGLINDE
(dicht an seinen Augen).

O lass in Nähe
zu dir mich neigen,
dass hell ich schaue
der dir aus Aug'
und Antlitz bricht,
und so süss die Sinne mir zwingt!

SIEGMUND.

Im Lenzesmond
leuchtest du hell;
hehr umwebt dich
das Wellenhaar;
was mich berückt,
errath' ich nun leicht —
denn wonnig weidet mein Blick.

SIEGLINDE
(schlägt ihm die Locken von der Stirn zurück und
betrachtet ihn staunend).

Wie dir die Stirn
so offen steht,
der Adern Geäst
in den Schläfen sich schlingt!
Mir zagt es vor der Wonne,
die mich entzückt —
ein Wunder will mich gemahnen: —
den heut' zuerst ich erschaut,
mein Auge sah dich schon!

SIEGMUND.

Ein Minnetraum
gemahnt auch mich:

Pressing thee, sweet, to my bosom—
Feeling thy heart as it beats!

SIEGLINDE.
(Starts in alarm and tears herself from his embrace.)
Ha! Who went? Who was it came?
(The outer door has opened wide. It remains open.
Outside the night is beautiful. The full moon shines
upon the two lovers, and all about them suddenly
becomes plainly visible.)

SIEGMUND.
(In gentle ecstacy.)
No one went—
Yet someone came.
See how the Spring
Smiles in the hall.
He draws her gently but firmly to him on the
couch.)
Winter's storming's stilled
By the love-lit May;
In tender beauty
Beameth the Spring.
On balmy breezes,
Light and lovely,
Weaving wonders,
See, he sways;
O'er wood and meadow
Softly breathing,
Wide he opes
His laughing eyes:
And happy birds are singing
Songs he taught,
Sweetest perfumes
Scent his train.
As he warms them, lo, the branches
Break into blossom;
Bud and bough
Submit to his sway.
In beauty's armor dight,
He witches the world.
Winter and storm vainly
Had said him nay:—
And even the surly portals
Obey his will, with the mortals
They fain would have barred
From—rapture and day.
To greet his sister,
Fast he has fared—
Twas Love that longed for the Spring.
In both our bosoms
Buried, lay Love:
But now she laughs in the light.
The bride who was sister
Is freed by the brother;
And shattered now
Lie barriers and chains.
Joyous greeting
Their lips exchange:
For Love has wed with the Spring!

SIEGLINDE.
Thou art the Spring

For whom I lay longing
And fasting through winter's frost;
'Twas thou my heart hailed
With holiest awe,
As thy look with love on me lighted.
Strange the world ever had seemed,
Friends had ne'er come to cheer me,
And all I counted as naught
That I met on my way.
But thee knew I,
Surely and soon;
When my glances met thine,
Mine thou wast only:
All my heart had once hid,
All I am,
Clear as the day
Now I could see:
The truth in mine ear
Sounded at last,
As in chill and dreary sorrow
A friend I in thee divined.
(She hangs upon his neck in rapture and looks
searchingly into his face.)

SIEGMUND.
O sweetest of raptures!
Woman divine!

SIEGLINDE.
(Gazing into his eyes.)
O let me nearer
To thee, dear, nestle,
For fain I'd gaze on
The holy light
That in thine eyes
And face doth shine,
And so sweetly draws me to thee.

SIEGMUND.
The love-lit moon
Glows in thy face;
Soft enfolds thee
Thy waving hair.
How I thy thrall
Became, know I well—
For rapture rivets my look.

SIEGLINDE.
(Brushes the hair back from his brow and looks at
him in amazement.)
Broad is thy brow,
And frank and fair,
Thy veins all entwined
In thy temples I trace.
I tremble, as my passion
Holds me enchained —
Some wonder thrills me with terror:—
Before I found thee to-night
Mine eyes thy face had seen!

SIEGMUND.
A dream of love,
I, too, recall.

in heissem Sehnen
sah ich dich schon!

SIEGLINDE.

Im Bach erblickt' ich
mein eigen Bild —
und jetzt gewahr' ich es wieder:
wie einst dem Teich es enttaucht,
bietest mein Bild mir nun du!

SIEGMUND.

Du bist das Bild —
das ich in mir barg

SIEGLINDE
(den Blick schnell abwendend).

O still! lass mich
der Stimme lauschen: —
mich dünkt, ihren Klang
hört' ich als Kind — —
doch nein! ich hörte sie neulich,
als meiner Stimme Schall
mir wiederhallte der Wald.

SIEGMUND.

O lieblichste Laute,
denen ich lausche!

SIEGLINDE
(schnell ihm wieder in's Auge spähend).

Deines Auges Gluth
erglänzte mir schon: —
so blickte der Greis
grüssend auf mich,
als der Traurigen Trost er gab.
An dem Blick
erkannt' ihn sein Kind —
schon wollt ich bei'm Namen ihn nennen
(Sie hält inne und fährt dann leise fort.)
Wehwalt heiss'st du fürwahr?

SIEGMUND.

Nicht heiss' mich so,
seit du mich liebst:
nun walt 'ich der hehrsten Wonnen!

SIEGLINDE.

Und Friedmund darfst du
froh dich nicht nennen?

SIEGMUND.

Nenne mich du,
wie du liebst, dass ich heisse:
den Namen nehm' ich von dir!

SIEGLINDE

Doch nanntest du Wolfe den Vater?

SIEGMUND.

Ein Wolf war er feigen Füchsen!
Doch dem so stolz
strahlte das Auge,
wie, Herrliche, hehr dir es strahlt,
der war — Wälse genannt.

SIEGLINDE
(ausser sich).

War Wälse dein Vater,
und bist du ein Wälsung,
stiess er für dich
sein Schwert in den Stamm —
so lass' mich dich heissen,
wie ich dich liebe:
Siegmund —
so nenn' ich dich.

SIEGMUND
(springt auf den Stamm zu und fasst den Schwe
griff).

Siegmund heiss' ich
und Siegmund bin ich:
bezeug' es dies Schwert,
das zaglos ich halte!
Wälse verhiess mir,
in höchster Noth
fänd' ich es einst:
ich fass' es nun!
Heiligster Minne
höchste Noth,
sehnender Liebe
sehrende Noth,
brennt mir hell in der Brust,
drängt zu That und Tod:
Nothung! Nothung! —
so nenn' ich dich, Schwert —
Nothung! Nothung!
neidlicher Stahl!
Zeig' deiner Schärfe
schneidenden Zahn:
heraus aus der Scheide zu mir!
(Er zieht mit einem gewaltigen Zuck das Schwe
aus dem Stamme und zeigt es der von Staunen un
Entzücken erfassten SIEGLINDE.)

Siegmund den Wälsung
Siehst du, Weib!
Als Brautgabe
bringt er dies Schwert:
so freit er sich
die seligste Frau:
dem Feindeshaus
entführt er dich so.
Fern von hier
folge ihm nun,
folge mir nun,
lachendes Haus:
dort schützt dich Nothung das Schwer
wenn Siegmund dir liebend erlag!
(Er umfasst sie, um sie mit sich fortzuziehen.)

SIEGLINDE
(in höchster Trunkenheit).

Eist du Siegmund,
den ich hier sehe —
Sieglinde bin ich,
die dich ersehnt:
die eig'ne Schwester
gewann'st du zueins mit dem Schwert!

I surely sought thee,
Wooed thee, ere now!

SIEGLINDE.
A brooklet mirrored
My face one morn—
And now again I behold it.
What once the water revealed
Now in thy face I can see!

SIEGMUND.
Thine is the face
That my heart had hid.

SIEGLINDE.
(Quickly averting her gaze.)
Ah, still! Let me
Thy voice recall, love!
Methinks, as a child,
Heard I it once—
Yet no! 'Twas lately I heard it,
When, echoing through the woods,
There came to me my own voice.

SIEGMUND.
How lovely the echoes
Sound as I listen!

SIEGLINDE.
(Again gazing into his eyes.)
Ah, those eyes of thine
Ere now I have seen.
So beamed on me once,
Cheering my grief,
The strange eyes of that agèd man.
By that glance
My father I found.
I nearly had named him by name.
(She pauses, and then goes on in a low voice):
"Woeful," surely I see?

SIEGMUND.
Not so I'm named
For thee, my love.
My world is all bliss and rapture.

SIEGLINDE.
And "Peaceful" none may
Call thee forever?

SIEGMUND.
Give me the name
That thy love would award me;
That name alone I will bear.

SIEGLINDE.
But was not thy father called Wolfè?

SIEGMUND.
Ay, Wolfè to dastard foxes!
Yet he whose eye
Shone with the lustre
That shines, O belovèd, in thine,
He was—Wälse, I ween.

SIEGLINDE.
(Beside herself.)
Thy father was Wälse?
Then thou art a Wälsung!
Fast in the tree
His sword for thee waits.
So let me re-name thee
As I do love thee:
Siegmund—
I thee proclaim!

SIEGMUND.
Siegmund, Victor,
Henceforth proclaim me.
Bear witness the sword
I grasp without shrinking.
Wälse foretold that,
In direst need,
Help it should bring—
I hold it now!
Love the most holy,
Direst need,
Loving and longing,
Sorest of need,
Burn and flame in my breast,
Drive to deeds and death.
Nothung! Needful!
Thou, sword, shalt be named—
Nothung! Nothung!
Blade of the brave!
Show me thy sharp
And shattering steel:
And—out of thy scabbard now leap!
(With a mighty tug he draws the sword from the
trunk and shows it to the astonished and delighted
SIEGLINDE.)
Siegmund the Wälsung,
Look, thou, wife!
Now brings to thee,
Bride, a true blade!
'Tis thus he woos
His dearest and best;
'Tis thus he frees
His love from her foe.
Far from here
Go where he goes,
Into the smiling
Sunshine of Spring,
Where Nothung aye shall keep guard
When Siegmund by love is disarmed!
(He puts his arm round her, to take her away with
him.)

SIEGLINDE.
(Ecstatically.)
Art thou Siegmund,
Here by my side?
Sieglinde am I,
For thee I sigh:
Thine own true sister
Thou'st won with the rape of the sword!

SIEGMUND.

Braut und Schwester
bist du dem Bruder —
so blühe denn Wälsungen-Blut!

(Er zieht sie mit wüthender Gluth an sich; sie sinkt
mit einem Schrei an seine Brust. — Der Vorhang
fällt schnell.)

ZWEITER AUFZUG.

Wildes Felsengebirg

Im Hintergrunde zieht sich von unten her eine
Schlucht herauf, die auf ein erhöhtes Felsjoch mün-
det; von diesem senkt sich der Boden dem Vordergrunde zu wieder abwärts.
WOTAN, kriegerisch gewaffnet und mit dem Speer:
vor ihm BRUENNHILDE, als WALKUERE, ebenfalls in voller Waffenrüstung.

WOTAN.

Nun zäume dein Ross,
reisige Maid!
Bald entbrennt
brünstiger Streit:
Brünnhilde stürme zum Streit,
dem Wälsung kiese sie Sieg!
Hunding wähle sich
wem er gehört:
nach Walhall taugt er mir nicht.
Drum rüstig und rasch
reite zur Wal!

BRUENNHILDE

(jauchzend von Fels zu Fels die Höhe rechts hinauf-
springend).

Hojotoho! Hojotoho!
Heiaha! Heiaha!
Hojotoho! Hojotoho!
Heiaha! Heiaha!
Hojotoho! Hojotoho!
Hojotoho! Hojotoho!
Heiahaha!
Hojotoho!

(Auf einer hohen Felsspitze hält sie an, blickt in
die hintere Schlucht hinab und ruft zu WOTAN zurück.)

Dir rath' ich, Vater,
rüste dich selbst;
harten Sturm
sollst du besteh'n:
Fricka naht, deine Frau,
im Wagen mit dem Widdergespann.
Hei! wie die gold'ne
Geissel sie schwingt;
die armen Thiere
ächzen vor Angst;
wild rasseln die Räder:
zornig fährt sie zum Zank!
In solchem Strausse
streit' ich nicht gern,
lieb' ich auch muthiger
Männer Schlacht:
drum sieh', wie den Sturm du bestehst;
ich Lustige lass' dich im Stich! —
Hojotoho! Hojotoho!

Heiaha! Heiaha!
Hojotoho! Hojotoho!
Heiaha! Heiaha!
Hojotoho! Hojotoho!
Hojotoho! Hojotoho!
Heiahaha!

(Sie ist hinter der Gebirgshöhe zur Seite verschwunden, während aus der Schlucht herauf FRICKA, in
einem mit zwei Widdern bespannten Wagen, auf dem
Joch anlangt: dort steigt sie schnell ab und schreitet
dann heftig in den Vordergrund auf WOTAN zu.)

WOTAN.

(indem er sie kommen sieht).

Der alte Sturm!
Die alte Müh'!
Doch Stand muss ich hier halten.

FRICKA.

Wo in Bergen du dich birgst
der Gattin Blick zu entgeh'n,
einsam hier
such' ich dich auf,
dass Hilfe du mir verhiessest.

WOTAN.

Was Fricka kümmert,
künde sie frei.

FRICKA.

Ich vernahm Hunding's Noth,
um Rache rief er mich an:
der Ehe Hüterin
hörte ihn,
verhiess streng
zu strafen die That
des frech frevelnden Paar's,
das kühn den Gatten gekränkt.

WOTAN.

Was so Schlimmes
schuf das Paar,
das liebend einte der Lenz?
Der Minne Zauber
entzückte sie:
wer büsst mir der Minne Macht?

FRICKA.

Wie thörig und taub du dich stellst,
als wüsstest fürwahr du nicht,
dass um der Ehe
heiligen Eid
den hart gekränkten, ich klage!

WOTAN.

Unheilig
acht' ich den Eid,
der Unliebende eint;
und mir wahrlich
muthe nicht zu,
dass mit Zwang ich halte,
was dir nicht haftet:
denn wo kühn Kräfte sich regen,
da rath' ich offen zum Krieg.

SIEGMUND.

Bride and sister
Be to thy brother—
So blest be thou, Wälsungen blood!

(**He** draws her to him rapturously. She falls on **his**
breast with a cry of ecstacy. Quick curtain.)

ACT TWO.

A Wild, Rocky Height.

In the background a wild ravine rises, leading to
a lofty and rocky height. The ground slopes down-
ward towards the foreground.
WOTAN is discovered in full armor and bearing his
spear. Before him stands BRÜNNHILDE, in the full
armor of a Walkyr.

WOTAN.

Now bridle thy steed,
Warfaring maid!
Soon shall come
Storming and strife.
Brünnhilde, haste to the fray,
The Wälsung surely must win.
Hunding's haven be
Here or be there—
Walhalla ne'er he shall see.
So up and away,
Haste to the field!

BRÜNNHILDE.

(Exalting, as she ascends the height on the right,
leaping from rock to rock.)

Ho-yo-to-ho! Ho-yo-to-ho!
Hi-ya-ha! Hi-ya-ha!
Ho-yo-to-ho! Ho-yc-to-ho!
Hi-ya-ha! Hi-ya-ha!
Ho-yo-to-ho! Ho-yo-to-ho!
Ho-yo-to-ho! Ho-yo-to-ho!
Hi-ya-ha-ha!
Ho-yo-to-ho!

(On reaching a high peak she halts, looks down into
the ravine beyond, and calls to WOTAN.)

I warn thee, father,
Armor thou'lt need:
Fierce the storm
Soon thou shalt meet.
Fricka cometh, thy wife,
She rideth in her car with the rams.
Ha! How her golden
Whip she doth crack!
Her team in terror
Trembles and moans!
Loud, loud the wheels rattle,
Wrath and war they forbode!
For such wild battles
Love have I none,
Joy though I may
In the strife of men!
So weather the storm as thou canst.
I laugh and I leave thee to fate!
Ho-yo-to-ho! Ho-yo-to-ho!

Hi-ya-ha! Hi-ya-ha!
Ho-yo-to-ho! Ho-yo-to-ho!
Hi-ya-ha! Hi-ya-ha!
Ho-yo-to-ho! Ho-yo-to-ho!
Ho-yo-to-ho! Ho-yo-to-ho!
Hi-ya-ha-ha!

(She vanishes behind the rocks, as FRICKA enters from
the heights, after ascending from the ravine, in a
chariot drawn by two rams, alights quickly, and strides
angrily towards WOTAN in the foreground.)

WOTAN.

(As he sees her coming.)

The old, old storm!
The old, old strife!
And yet here I must face her!

FRICKA.

On the hill-side thou dost hide,
My wifely eyes to evade.
Here come I,
Riding alone,
To seek the help thou didst promise.

WOTAN.

Thy troubles, Fricka,
Freely unfold!

FRICKA.

Now I know Hunding's need:
For vengeance rightly he prayed.
And I, who watch over
Married love,
Stand pledged
Now to punish the wrong
A bold, brazen-faced pair
Have wrought against one who's wed.

WOTAN.

Was the evil
Done so dire
By those the Spring had made one?
The magic meshes
Of love accuse:
Nor count it a crime to love.

FRICKA.

How dull and how deaf thou wouldst
seem,
As though it were truly strange
That in defence
Of holiest bonds,
I take up arms for the wronged one!

WOTAN.

Unholy
Deem I the oath
That unloving is sworn:
And wouldst thou, then,
Have me hold chain'd
Those whom thou hast striven
In vain to fetter?
For where such fires fiercely are raging
My rede is—stay not the flames.

FRICKA.

Achtest du rühmlich
der Ehe Bruch,
so prahle nun weiter
und preis' es heilig,
dass Blutschande entblüht
dem Bund eines Zwillingpaar's.
Mir schaudert das Herz,
es schwindelt mein Hirn:
bräutlich umfing
die Schwester der Bruder.
Wann — ward es erlebt,
dass leiblich Geschwister sich liebten?

WOTAN.

Heut' — hast du's erlebt:
erfahre so,
was von selbst sich fügt,
sei zuvor auch noch nie es gescheh'n.
Dass jene sich lieben,
leuchtet dir hell:
drum höre redlichen Rath!
Soll süsse Lust
deinen Segen dir lohnen,
so seg'ne, lachend der Liebe,
Siegmund's und Sieglinde's Bund!

FRICKA
(in höchste Entrüstung ausbrechend).

So ist es denn aus
mit den ewigen Göttern,
seit du die wilden
Wälsungen zeugtest?
Heraus sagt' ich's —
traf ich den Sinn?
Nichts gilt dir der Hehren
heilige Sippe;
hin wirfst du Alles,
was einst du geachtet;
zerreissest die Bande,
die selbst du gebunden;
lösest lachend
des Himmels Haft —
dass nach Lust und Laune nur walte
dies frevelnde Zwillingspaar,
deiner Untreue zuchtlose Frucht! —
O, was klag' ich
um Ehe und Eid,
du zuerst du selbst sie versehrt!
Die treue Gattin
trogest du stets:
wo eine Tiefe,
wo eine Höhe,
dahin lugte
lüstern dein Blick,
wie des Wechsels Lust du gewännest,
und höhnend kränktest mein Herz!
Trauernden Sinnes
musst' ich's ertragen,

zog'st du zur Schlacht
mit den schlimmen Mädchen,
die wilder Minne
Bund dir gebar;
denn dein Weib noch scheutest du so,
dass der Walküren Schaar,
und Brünnhilde selbst,
deines Wunsches Braut,
in Gehorsam der Herrin du gab'st.
Doch jetzt, da dir neue
Namen gefielen,
als "Wälse" wölfisch
im Walde du schweiftest;
jetzt, da zu niedrigster
Schmach du dich neigtest,
gemeiner Menschen
ein Paar zu erzeugen:
jetzt dem Wurfe der Wölfin
wirfst du zu Füssen dein Weib! —
So führ' es denn aus,
fülle das Mass:
die Betrog'ne lass auch zertreten!

WOTAN
(ruhig).

Nichts lerntest du,
wollt' ich dich lehren,
was nie du erkennen kannst,
eh' nicht ertagte die That.
Stets Gewohntes
nur magst du versteh'n:
doch was noch nie sich traf,
darnach trachtet mein Sinn!
Eines höre!
Noth thut ein Held,
der, ledig göttlichen Schutzes,
sich löse vom Göttergesetz:
so nur taugt er
zu wirken die That,
die, wie noth sie den Göttern,
dem Gott doch zu wirken verwehrt

FRICKA.

Mit tiefem Sinne
willst du mich täuschen!
Was Hehres sollten
Helden je wirken,
das ihren Göttern wäre verwehrt
deren Gunst in ihnen nur wirkt?

WOTAN.

Ihres eignen Muthes
achtest du nicht?

FRICKA.

Wer hauchte Menschen ihn ein?
Wer hellte den Blöden den Blick?
In deinem Schutz
scheinen sie stark,
durch deinen Stachel

FRICKA.

Since thou dost honor
The crime I hate,
Go further in folly,
Proclaim it holy,
Where incest is the fruit
Of love between two born twins.
Aghast is my heart,
A-whirl is my brain:
Wedded, they twain,
The sister and brother!
Whene'er was it known
That brother and sister were mated?

WOTAN.

Now—here it is known:
And so be sure
That it had to be,
Though till now it had never yet been.
They love one another,
Surely 'tis plain:
So yield to reason and rede.
Let bliss be born
Of the love that thou sealest,
And laugh to know thou art blessing
Siegmund and Sieglinde's bond.

FRICKA.
(In a storm of indignation.)
To this has it come
With the gods everlasting,
Since thou the lawless
Wälsungs begottest?
My shaft went home—
Straight to the mark?
Naught holy thou holdest,
Kinship nor Godhead:
Away thou flingest
The laws thou didst honor;
Destroyest the fetters
That came of thy forging;
Mock thou makest
Of Heav'n's behest—
That the sinful sister and brother
May love in their own wild way.
And thy faithlessness bore the bad fruit!
But why fret over
Weddings and vows
That thyself did first laugh to scorn?
Thy wife so faithful
Aye thou didst wrong!
Is there a valley,
Is there a mountain,
Thine eye, lusting,
Hath not profaned?
As thy love of change became stronger,
More harrowed e'er was my heart!
What did my mourning
Mean to thy pleasure?

Forth thou wouldst fare
With the wicked maidens,
Of love untrammelled
Born for thy bane.
Yet thy wife at least thou didst dread,
For Brünnhild' herself,
Best lov'd of them all,
With thy Walkyr band,
Thou didst order my will to obey,
But now, since disguises
New did delight thee;
Since wolfish "Wälse"
In woods went a-roaming;
Now that the nethermost
Depth thou hast fathomed,
Begetting, shameless,
A brace of mere mortals;
Now thy wife thou wouldst offer
Up to the whelps of thy dam?
Well, go thine own way,
Halt at no shame,
Let them crush me, too, in their triumph!

WOTAN.
(Calmly.)
Naught thou wouldst learn,
Though I should teach thee
What never thy mind could grasp
Till what must happen shall be.
What is common
Alone thou canst read:
But what ne'er yet was known
In my mind I foresee.
Mark this only!
One there must come,
A hero, slighted of heaven,
The laws of the Gods to defy.
That would fit him
To do the great deed
Not a God in Walhalla
Would dare, though the need should be
dire.

FRICKA.
Thy words and wisdom
Would but deceive me.
What deed could heroes
Work that were worthy,
Where we, the gods almighty, had failed?
By our grace alone do they work.

WOTAN.
Dost thou count their courage
Truly for naught?

FRICKA.
Who gave that courage to men?
Who opened their eyes to the light?
With thee for shield,
Strong they may seem.
With thee to spur them,

streben sie auf:
du — reizest sie einzig
die so mir Ew'gen du rühmst.
    Mit neuer List
    willst du mich belügen,
    durch neue Ränke
    jetzt mir entrinnen;
    doch diesen Wälsung
    gewinnst du dir nicht:
in ihm treff' ich nur dich,
denn durch dich trotzt er allein.

WOTAN.
    In wilden Leiden
    erwuchs er sich selbst:
mein Schutz schirmte ihn nie.

FRICKA.
So schütz' auch heut' ihn nicht;
    nimm ihm das Schwert,
    das du ihm geschenkt!

WOTAN.
    Das Schwert?

FRICKA.
    Ja — das Schwert,
    das zauberstark
    zuckende Schwert,
das du Gott dem Sohne gab'st.

WOTAN.
    Siegmund gewann es sich
    selbst in der Noth.

FRICKA.
    Du schuf'st ihm die Noth;
    wie das neidliche Schwert:
    willst du mich täuschen,
    die Tag und Nacht
    auf den Fersen dir folgt?
    Für ihn stiessest du
    das Schwert in den Stamm;
    du verhiessest ihm
    die hehre Wehr:
    willst du es leugner.,
    dass nur deine List
    ihn lockte, wo er es fänd'?
    (WOTAN macht eine Geberde des Grimmes.)
    Mit Unfreien
    streitet kein Edler,
den Frevler straft nur der Freie:
    wider deine Kraft
    führt' ich wohl Krieg;
doch Siegmund verfiel mir als Knecht.
    (WOTAN wendet sich unmuthig ab.)
    Der dir als Herren
    hörig und eigen
    gehorchen soll ihm
    dein ewig Gemahl?
    Soll mich in Schmach
    der Niedrigste schmähen,

    dem Frechen zum Sporn,
    dem Freien zum Spott?
Das kann mein Gatte nicht wollen,
die Göttin entweiht er nicht so!

WOTAN
(finster).
Was verlangst du?

FRICKA.
Lass' von dem Wälsung!

WOTAN
(mit gedämpfter Stimme).
Er geh' seines Weg's.

FRICKA.
Doch du — schütze ihn nicht,
wenn zur Schlacht der Rächer ihn ruft!

WOTAN.
Ich — schütze ihn nicht.

FRICKA.
    Sieh' mir in's Auge,
    sinne nicht Trug!
Die Walküre wend' auch von ihm!

WOTAN.
Die Walküre walte frei!

FRICKA.
    Nicht doch! Deinen Willen
    vollbringt sie allein:
verbiete ihr Siegmund's Sieg!

WOTAN
(mit heftigem innerem Kampfe).
Ich kann ihn nicht fällen:
er fand mein Schwert!

FRICKA.
    Entzieh' dem den Zauber,
    zerknick' es dem Knecht:
schutzlos find' ihn der Feind!

BRUENNHILDE'S VOICE.
    Heiaha! Heiaha!
    Hojotoho!
(Sie vernimmt von der Höhe her den jauchzenden
Walkürenruf BRUENNHILDE'S: diese erscheint dann
dann selbst mit ihrem Ross auf dem Felspfade rechts.

FRICKA.
Dort kommt deine kühne Maid:
jauchzend jagt sie daher.

BRUENNHILDE'S VOICE.
    Heiaha! Heiaha!
    Hojohotojohotojoha!

WOTAN
(dumpf für sich).
Ich rief sie für Siegmund zu Ross.

FRICKA.
    Deiner ew'gen Gattin
    heilige Ehre
beschirme heut' ihr Schild!

Well they may strive.
Thou—only dost goad them,
These men whose praise thou dost sing.
With new deceit
Wouldest thou beguile me;
With new devices
Wouldest thou evade me;
But this one Wälsung
No cunning shall save.
In him thyself I strike.
'Twas thy might made him so brave.

WOTAN.

In pain and sorrow
Alone was he reared:
My shield shelter ne'er gave.

FRICKA.

Then shieldless let him stand;
Take back the sword,
That to thee he owes.

WOTAN.

The sword?

FRICKA.

Ay—the sword,
The magical,
Masterful sword,
Thou, a god, didst give thy son.

WOTAN.

Siegmund has conquer'd it,
Won it in need.

FRICKA.

Thou madest the need,
When he needed the sword;
Wouldst thou deceive me
Who, night and day,
In thy traces have trod?
For him didst thou thrust
The sword in the tree;
Ay, the noble blade
Was meant for him.
Wilt thou deny
That thy cunning alone
Allured him where it was found?
(WOTAN knits his brows wrathfully.)
Can gods join
In battle with bondsmen?
The guilty should they but punish.
Braving thee, so strong,
War I might wage;
But Siegmund is only my thrall.
(WOTAN turns away impatiently.)
Shall he who owes thee
Duty and homage
Be master now
To the wife thou hast wed?
Shall he, a clod,
Put shame on thy goddess —

The base-born be lord —
The mighty be scorned?
Ah, no! My lord cannot wish it —
His goddess he would not degrade!

WOTAN.
(Gloomily.)
What, then, wouldst thou?

FRICKA.

Cast off the Wälsung!

WOTAN.
(Lowering his voice.)
His weird he shall dree!

FRICKA.

But thou — shelter him not,
When the foeman his vengeance seeks!

WOTAN.

I'll — not be his shield.

FRICKA.

Face me more frankly —
Think not of fraud.
The Walkyr must lend him no aid!

WOTAN.

The Walkyrie fareth free.

FRICKA.

Not so! As thou willest
She comes and she goes.
Forbid her to let him win!

WOTAN.
(Fighting against his emotion.)
I cannot undo him:
He wields my sword!

FRICKA.

Then kill thou its magic:
'Twill break in his hand —
Helpless finds him his foe!

BRÜNNHILDE'S VOICE.

Hi-ya-ha! Hi-ya-ha!
Ho-yo-to-ho!
(From the heights she hears the jubilant Walkyr
cry of BRÜNNHILDE, who appears soon after with her
steed on the rocky path, to the right.)

FRICKA.

Here hastens thy daring maid —
Joyful hither she hies!

BRÜNNHILDE'S VOICE.

Hi-ya-ha! Hi-ya-ha!
Ho-yo-ho-to-yo-ho-to-yo-ha!

WOTAN.
(Aside.)
For Siegmund she saddled her steed!

FRICKA.

To protect the spotless
Fame of thy goddess
See thou her shield doth shine!

Von Menschen verlacht,
verlustig der Macht,
gingen wir Götter zu Grund,
würde heut' nicht hehr
und herrlich mein Recht
geräcät von der muthigen Maid. —
Der Wälsung fällt meiner Ehre: —
empfah' ich von Wotan den Eid?

WOTAN
(in furchtbarem Unmuth und innerem Grimm auf einen Felsensitz sich werfend).

Nimm den Eid!

(Als Brünnhilde von der Höhe aus Fricka gewahrte, brach sie schnell ihren Gesang ab, und hat nun still und langsam ihr Ross am Zügel den Felsweg herabgeleitet; sie birgt dieses jetzt in einer Höhle, als Fricka, zu ihrem Wagen sich zurückwendend, an ihr vorbeischreitet.)

FRICKA.
(zu BRUENNHILDE).

Heervater
harret dein:
lass' ihn dir künden,
wie das Loos er gekies't!
(Sie besteigt den Wagen und fährt schnell nach hinten davon.)

BRUENNHILDE
(tritt mit verwunderter und besorgter Miene vor WOTAN, der, auf dem Felssitz zurückgelehnt das auf die Hand gestützt, in finsteres Brüten versunken ist).

Schlimm, fürcht' ich,
schloss der Streit,
lachte Fricka dem Loose! —
Vater, was soll
dein Kind erfahren?
Trübe scheinst du und traurig!

WOTAN
(lässt den Arm machtlos sinken und den Kopf in den Nacken fallen).

In eig'ner Fessel
fing ich mich: —
ich unfreiester Aller!

BRUENNHILDE

So sah ich dich nie!
Was nagt dir das Herz?

WOTAN
(in wildem Ausbruche den Arm erhebend).

O heilige Schmach!
O schmählicher Harm!
Götternoth!
Götternoth!
Endloser Grimm!
Ewiger Gram!
Der Traurigste bin ich von Allen!

BRUENNHILDE
(wirft erschrocken Schild, Speer und Helm von sich, und lässt sich mit besorgter Zutraulichkeit zu WOTAN'S Füssen nieder).

Vater! Vater!
Sage, was ist dir?
Was erschreck'st du mit Sorge dein
Kind!

Vertraue mir:
ich bin dir treu;
sieh', Brünnhilde bittet!
(Sie legt traulich und ängstlich Haupt und Hände ihm auf Knie und Schooss.)

WOTAN
(blickt ihr lange in's Auge und streichelt ihr dann die Locken: wie aus tiefem Sinnen zu sich kommend, beginnt er endlich mit sehr leiser Stimme).

Lass' ich's verlauten,
lös' ich dann nicht
meines Willens haltenden Haft?

BRUENNHILDE
(ihm eben so leise erwidernd).

Zu Wotan's Willen sprichst du,
sagst du mir, was du willst:
wer — bin ich,
wär' ich dein Wille nicht?

WOTAN

Was Keinem in Worten ich künde,
unausgesprochen
bleib' es denn ewig:
mit mir nur rath' ich,
red' ich zu dir. — — —
(Mit noch gedämpfterer, schauerlicher Stimme, während er BRUENNHILDEN unverwandt in das Auge blickt.)

Als junger Liebe
Lust mir verblich,
verlangte nach Macht mein Mund:
von jäher Wünsche
Wüthen gejagt,
gewann ich mir die Welt.
Unwissend trugvoll
Untreue übt' ich,
band durch Verträge,
was Unheil barg:
listig verlockte mich Loge,
der schweifend nun verschwand.
Von der Liebe doch
mocht' ich nicht lassen;
in der Macht verlangt' ich nach Minne,
den Nacht gebar,
der bange Nibelung,
Alberich brach ihren Bund,
er fluchte der Liebe,
und gewann durch den Fluch
des Rheines glänzendes Gold
und mit ihm masslose Macht.
Den Ring, den er schuf,
entriss ich ihm listig:
doch nicht dem Rhein
gab ich ihn zurück;
mit ihm bezahlt' ich
Walhall's Zinnen,
der Burg, die Riesen mir bauten,
aus der ich der Welt nun gebot.
Die Alles weiss,
was einstens war,
Erda, die weihlich

To mortals a mock,
And stripp'd of our might,
Gods though we be, we were doomed,
Should the warrior maid
To-day but betray
My rightful and holiest cause.
The Wälsung dies for my honor:
Does Wotan so pledge me his oath?

WOTAN.
(Raging and inwardly wrathful, as he throws himself
on a rocky seat.)
Take mine oath!
(BRÜNNHILDE, perceiving FRICKA, has suddenly inter-
rupted her song and has led her steed slowly and
silently down the rocky path. She hides the steed in
a cave, just as FRICKA passes her on her way back to
her chariot.)

FRICKA.
(To BRÜNNHILDE.)
War-lord, he
Waits for thee:
He will inform thee
How his lot he has cast!
(She gets into her chariot and is driven off quickly
in the background.)

BRÜNNHILDE.
(Moves toward WOTAN, looking anxious and amazed.
WOTAN reclines on his rocky seat, resting his head on
his hand. He is brooding gloomily.)
Ill, surely,
Ends the strife —
Fricka laughed as she left us!
Father, what shall
Thy child discover?
Sad thou seemest and solemn!

WOTAN.
(Lets his arm drop limply and bows his head.)
I forged the fetters.
Chain'd I stand —
I, most bound of all bondsmen!

BRÜNNHILDE.
Thus ne'er thou didst look.
What gnaws at thy heart?

WOTAN.
(Raising his arm in violent excitement.)
How awful the shame!
How shameful this woe!
Cursèd we!
Gods! Accurst!
Endless the grief!
Endless the groans!
Ah, saddest of all, I lie mourning!

BRÜNNHILDE.
(In alarm, throwing away her shield, spear and hel-
met, and kneeling affectionately at WOTAN's feet)
Father! Father!
Tell me, what ails thee?
See what terror bewilders thy child!

Have trust in me—
To thee I'm true—
See, Brünnhilde begs thee!
(She lays her head and hands trustingly but distress-
fully on his knee.)

WOTAN.
(Gazes long into her face and strokes her hair. Then,
as if coming to himself again, he at last begins in a
very low voice.)
Did I reveal it,
Should I not lose
What is left of might in my will?

BRÜNNHILDE.
(Answering in an equally low voice.)
To Wotan's will thou speakest:
Tell me now what thou wilt.
What—were I,
Could I thy will not be?

WOTAN.
What never in words had been fashioned,
Unuttered still
Shall be, and for ever.
Myself I speak to,
Speaking to thee. — — —
(In a more subdued and awestruck voice, looking
fixedly at BRÜNNHILDE.)
As Love's young fancy
Faded and died,
I longed for the pride of power:
A-flame with olden
Wishes, I went
To win the whole wide world.
Untried, yet artful,
Falsehood I fostered,
Bargained and ordered
What ill should bring.
Luring me lower came Loge,
No sooner come than gone.
But my lust for delight
Was unsated;
In my power, for passion I panted.
'Twas Night that bore
The fearsome Nibelung,
Alberich; mocking my plans,
And cursing all love,
With his curses he won
The glittering gold of the Rhine,
And with it, measureless might.
The ring which he wrought
I ravished by cunning:
But still bereft
Did the Rhine remain:
The gold I gave for
Walhall's ramparts,
The stronghold reared by the giants,
From which the whole world I should
rule.
She who knows all
That e'er has been,
Erda, most wise

weiseste Wala,
rieth mir ab von dem Ring,
warnte vor ewigem Ende.
 Von dem Ende wollt' ich
 mehr noch wissen;
doch schweigend entschwand mir das
        Weib.
Da verlor ich den leichten Muth;
zu wissen begehrt es den Gott:
 in den Schoos der Welt
 schwang ich mich hinab,
 mit Liebes-Zauber
 zwang ich die Wala,
stört' ihres Wissens Stolz,
dass sie Rede nun mir stand.
Kunde empfing ich von ihr:
von mir doch barg sie ein Pfand:
der Welt weisestes Weib
gebar mir, Brünnhilde, dich.
 Mit acht Schwestern
 zog ich dich auf:
 durch euch Walküren
 wollt' ich wenden,
 was mir die Wala
 zu fürchten schuf —
ein schmähliches Ende der Ew'gen.
 Dass stark zum Streit
 uns fände der Feind,
hiess ich euch Helden mir schaffen:
 die herrisch wir sonst
 in Gesetzen hielten,
 die Männer, denen
 den Muth wir gewehrt,
 die durch trüber Verträge
 trügende Bande
 zu blindem Gehorsam
 wir uns gebunden —
 die solltet zu Sturm
 und Streit ihr nun stacheln,
 ihre Kraft reizen
 zu rauhem Krieg,
dass kühner Kämpfer Schaaren
ich sammle in Walhall's Saal.

BRUENNHILDE.
Deinen Saal füllten wir weidlich;
viele schon führt' ich dir zu.
 Was macht dir nun Sorge,
 da nie wir gesäumt?

WOTAN.
 Ein Andres ist's:
 achte es wohl,
wess' mich die Wala gewarnt! —
 Durch Alberich's Heer
 droht uns das Ende:
 mit neidischem Grimm
 grollt mir der Niblung;
 doch scheu' ich nun nicht
 seine nächtigen Schaaren —

meine Helden schüfen mir Sieg.
 Nur wenn je den Ring
 zurück er gewänne —
dann wäre Walhall verloren:
 der der Liebe fluchte,
 er allein
 nützte neidisch
 des Ringes Runen
 zu aller Edlen
 endlosen Schmach;
 der Helden Muth
 entwendet er mir;
 die Kühnen selber
 zwäng' er zum Kampf,
 mit ihrer Kraft
 bekriegte er mich.
Sorgend sann ich nun selbst,
den Ring dem Feind zu entreissen:
 der Riesen einer,
 denen ich einst
 mit verfluchtem Gold
 den Fleiss vergalt,
Fafner hütet den Hort,
um den er den Bruder gefällt.
Ihm müsst' ich den Reif entringen,
den selbst als Zoll ich ihm zahlte:
 doch mit dem ich vertrug
 ihn darf ich nicht treffen;
 machtlos vor ihm
 erläge mein Muth.
 Das sind die Bande,
 die mich binden:
der durch Verträge ich Herr,
den Verträgen bin ich nun Knecht.
 Nur Einer könnte,
 was ich nicht darf:
 ein Held, dem helfend
 nie ich mich neigte;
 der fremd dem Gotte,
 frei seiner Gunst,
 unbewusst,
 ohne Geheiss,
 aus eig'ner Noth
 mit der eig'nen Wehr
 schüfe die That,
 die ich scheuen muss,
die nie mein Rath ihm rieth,
wünscht sie auch einzig mein Wunsch!
 Der entgegen dem Gott
 für mich föchte,
 den freundlichen Feind,
 wie fände ich ihn?
Wie schüf' ich den Freien,
 den nie ich schirmte,
 der in eig'nem Trotze
 der Trauteste mir?
Wie macht' ich den Andren,
 der nicht mehr ich,
 und aus sich wirkte,

And womanly Wala,
Warned me off from the ring,
Bade me beware of disaster.
Of the end I begged her
    More to tell me.
But silent she faded from sight.
Then my courage at last I lost;
For knowledge a god was a-thirst.
    In the womb of Earth
    Sought I now for light;
    With magic love, I
    Mastered the Wala,
Wrung from her wisdom's pride
What I longed so sore to know.
What had been dark, she made clear,
Yet hid a pledge from mine eyes:
    The world's Wala, most wise,
    Did bear me, Brünnhilde, thee.
    With eight sisters
    Thee did I rear:
    With ye Walkyrs, I
    Sought escape
    From what erst the Wala
    Had bid me dread—
The end of the gods everlasting.
    To make us strong
    In strife with the foe,
Sent I ye searching for heroes:
    The men whom we once
With our laws held tightly,
    The men whose courage
    And strength we had stol'n,
Whom with compacts our cunning
Surely had fettered,
    And bound to obey us
    For good or evil—
    'Twas these ye should spur
    To storm and to striving,
    Aye their hearts steeling
    To dare and do,
    Till hosts of warriors mighty
Should stand in Walhalla's hall.

BRÜNNHILDE.

And thy hall fast we are filling;
Many I've borne to thine aid.
Then why dost thou sorrow,
When we are so true?

WOTAN.

There's more behind—
Hear me and heed—
Whereof the Wala has warned!—
    'Tis Alberich's host
    Comes to undo us:
    The Nibelung's hate
    Rankles and threatens.
    Yet have I no fear
Of his dark and grim forces—

With my heroes, victor I'd be.
    But should he the ring
    I ravished recover—
Then were Walhall lost forever.
    He who cursed all loving,
    He alone,
    Dreams of using
    Its runes to compass
    The shameful ruin
    Set for the gods.
    He seeks to steal
    My heroes away:
    My boldest warriors
    Fain he would win.
    And with their might
    He'd master e'en me.
Soon a scheme I devised
To wrest the ring from his clutches.
    The giant Fafner,
    Once I had paid
    With accursèd gold
    Walhall to raise:
Now the treasure he guards
For which he his brother had slain.
From him must the ring be wrested
That erst he'd earned with his valor.
    But with him I am leagued,
    Nor could I attack him;
    Strike though I would,
    My stroke were in vain.
    These are the fetters
    That enchain me:
I who had fashioned the snare,
Now am caught and held in the toils.
    Yet one might venture
    Where I am weak:
    A hero whom I
    Never had succored;
    Whom ne'er with favors
    Gods had enchained,
    All unurged,
    Bound by no bond,
    Himself to save,
    With his own strong sword
    Surely could dare
    What I dare not do,
What ne'er by word I'd willed,
Warm though my wish might have been.
    Who, opposing the god,
    Should yet help him,
    A friend, though a foe—
    Ah, where doth he hide?
    How fashion the freeman
    Whom ne'er I shielded,
    Who, a seeming rebel,
    Were dearest to me?
    How could I create him
    Who'd not be I,
    And yet were willing

was ich nur will? —
O göttliche Noth!
Grässliche Schmach!
Zum Ekel find' ich
ewig nur mich
in Allem, was ich erwirke!
Das And're, das ich ersehne,
das And're erseh' ich nie;
denn selbst muss der Freie sich schaffen —
Knechte erknet' ich mir nur!

BRUENNHILDE.

Doch der Wälsung, Siegmund?
wirkt er nicht selbst?

WOTAN

Wild durchschweift' ich
mit ihm die Wälder;
gegen der Götter Rath
reizte kühn ich ihn auf —
gegen der Götter Rache
schützt ihn nun einzig das Schwert,
das eines Gottes
Gunst ihm beschied —
Wie wollt' ich listig
selbst mich belügen?
So leicht ja entfrug mir
Fricka den Trug!
Zu tiefster Scham
durchschaute sie mich:
ihrem Willen muss ich gewähren!

BRUENNHILDE.

So nimmst du von Siegmund den Sieg?

WOTAN

(in wildem Schmerz der Verzweiflung ausbrechend).
Ich berührte Alberich's Ring —
gierig hielt ich das Gold!
Der Fluch, den ich floh,
nicht flieht er nun mich: —
was ich liebe, muss ich verlassen,
morden, wen je ich minne,
trügend verrathen,
wer mir vertraut! —
Fahre denn hin,
herrische Pracht,
göttlichen Prunkes
prahlende Schmach!
Zusammen breche,
was ich gebaut!
Auf geb' ich mein Werk,
Nur eines will ich noch,
das Ende — —
das Ende! —
(Er hält sinnend ein.)
Und für das Ende
sorgt Alberich! —
jetzt versteh' ich
den stummen Sinn

des wilden Wortes der Wala: —
"Wenn der Liebe finstrer Feind
zürnend zeugt einen Sohn,
der Seligen Ende
säumt dann nicht!" —
Vom Niblung jüngst
vernahm ich die Mähr',
dass ein Weib der Zwerg bewältigt,
dess' Gunst Gold ihm erzwang.
Des Hasses Frucht
hegt eine Frau;
des Neides Kraft
kreiss't ihr im Schoosse:
das Wunder gelang
dem Liebelosen:
doch der in Lieb' ich frei'te,
den Freien erlang' ich mir nicht! —
(Grimmig.)
So nimm meinen Segen,
Niblungen-Sohn!
Was tief mich ekelt,
dir geb' ich's zum Erbe,
der Gottheit nichtigen Glanz;
zernage ihn gierig dein Neid!

BRUENNHILDE
(erschrocken).

O sag', künde!
Was soll nun dein Kind?

WOTAN
(bitter).

Fromm streite für Fricka,
hüte ihr Eh' und Eid'!
Was sie erkor,
das kiese auch ich.
Was frommte mir eig'ner Wille?
Einen Freien kann ich nicht wollen —
für Fricka's Knechte
kämpfe nun du!

BRUENNHILDE.

Weh! nimm reuig
zurück das Wort!
Du liebst Siegmund:
dir zu Lieb' —
ich weiss es — schütz' ich den Wälsung

WOTAN.

Fällen sollst du Siegmund,
für Hunding erfechten den Sieg!
Hüte dich wohl
und halte dich stark;
all deiner Kühnheit
entbiete im Kampf:
ein Sieg-Schwert
schwingt Siegmund —
schwerlich fällt er dir feig.

BRUENNHILDE.

Den du zu lieben
stets mich gelehrt,

To work my will?
O shame on the gods!
Sorrow and shame!
To mock me always,
Only I find
Myself in all I am planning!
The man for whom I am longing,
That hero I ne'er shall see;
For freemen themselves must give life
    to—
Thralls all my creatures would be!

BRÜNNHILDE.
But the Wälsung, Siegmund?
Is he not free?

WOTAN.
Once, together
We roamed the forest;
Ever against the gods
Strove he, as was my rede.
Now from the wrathful goddess
Shelters him naught but the sword—
And that my favor
Sent in his need.
For all my cunning
Could not conceal it—
So easily Fricka
Found out the lie.
She read me through
And filled me with shame:
Though I would, I could not resist her!

BRÜNNHILDE.
So Siegmund is doomed to defeat?

WOTAN.
(In a frenzy of despair.)
I have handled Alberich's ring—
Grasped with greed at the gold!
The curse that I fled
Now clingeth to me:—
What I love, perforce I abandon,
Slay, when I'd fain be saving:
Traitor I turn
To him who trusts!—
Fare ye then well,
Lordship and pride,
Godhead and glory
Buried in shame!
So now must perish
All I had wrought!
Farewell to my work
Soon will my pomp and I
Be ended— —
Be ended!—
(Pauses in meditation.)
And 'twill be ended
By Alberich!—
Now I fathom
What once had hid

The whirling words of the Wala:—
"When the grimmest foe of love,
Fiercely fathers a son,
The gods immortal
Near their end!"
    A wondrous tale
    I've heard of the Dwarf
Who had won a greedy woman,
With gold blinding her eyes.
    The fruit of hate
    Soon shall be seen;
    The envious germ
    Bursts into life:
    The wonder was wrought
    By loveless lovers:
But I, who loved so fondly,
The freeman I never can see!—
    (Grimly.)
    Then take thou my blessing,
    Nibelung-born!
    My shame and sorrow
    I gladly will give thee.
My godship's meaningless might
Thy malice may have when it will!

BRÜNNHILDE.
(In terror.)
O speak quickly—
What must I then do?

WOTAN.
(Bitterly.)
Go! Fight thou for Fricka,
See to her wedding vows!
    As she has chos'n,
    I, also, must choose.
What good were now all my willing?
With my will I ne'er made a freeman—
    For Fricka's bondsmen
    Battle now do!

BRÜNNHILDE.
Woe! My father,
Call back thy words!
Dost love Siegmund?
Then for thee—
For thy sake—shield I the Wälsung!

WOTAN.
Siegmund shalt thou slaughter;
'Tis Hunding must win in the fray!
    Watch thyself well—
    Thy strength do not waste;
    All of thy prowess
    Thou'lt need in the fight:
    A strong sword
    Swings Siegmund—
Surely brave he will be.

BRÜNNHILDE.
Him thou hast taught me
    Alway to love,

der in hehrer Tugend
dem Herzen dir theuer —
gegen ihn zwingt mich nimmer
dein zwiespältig Wort.

WOTAN

Ha, Freche, du!
frevelst du mir?
Wer bist du, als meines Willens
blind wählende Kür? —
da mit dir ich tagte,
sank ich so tief,
dass zum Schimpf der eig'nen
Geschöpfe ich ward?
Kennst du Kind, meinen Zorn?
Verzage dein Muth,
wenn je zermalmend
auf dich stürzte sein Strahl!
In meinem Busen
berg' ich den Grimm,
der in Grau'n und Wust
wirft eine Welt,
die einst zur Lust mir gelacht: —
wehe dem, den er trifft!
Trauer schüf' ihm sein Trotz! —
Drum rath' ich dir,
reize mich nicht;
besorge was ich befahl: —
Siegmund falle! —
Dies sei der Walküre Werk.
(Er stürmt fort, und verschwindet schnell links im
Gebirge.)

BRUENNHILDE
(steht lange betäubt und erschrocken.)

So — sah ich
Siegvater nie,
erzürnt' ihn sonst wohl auch ein Zank!
(Sie neigt sich betrübt und nimmt ihre Waffen auf,
mit denen sie sich wieder rüstet.)
Schwer wiegt mir
der Waffen Wucht: —
wenn nach Lust ich focht,
wie waren sie leicht! —
Zu böser Schlacht
schleich' ich heut' so bang! —
(Sie sinnt, und seufzt dann auf.)
Weh', mein Wälsung!
Im höchsten Leid
muss dich treulos die Treue verlassen!
(Sie wendet sich nach hinten, und gewahrt SIEG-
MUND und SIEGLINDE, wie sie aus der Schlucht
heraufsteigen: sie betrachtet die Nahenden einen
Augenblick und wendet sich dann in die Höhle zu
ihrem Ross, so dass sie dem Zuschauer gänzlich verschwindet.)

(SIEGMUND und SIEGLINDE treten auf. Sie
schreitet hastig voraus; er sucht sie aufzuhalten.)

SIEGMUND.

Raste nun hier:
gönne dir Ruh'!

SIEGLINDE.

Weiter! weiter!

SIEGMUND
(umfasst sie mit sanfter Gewalt).

Nicht weiter nun!
Verweile, süssestes Weib! —
Aus Wonne-Entzücken
zucktest du auf,
mit jäher Hast
jagtest du fort;
kaum folgt' ich der wilden Flucht:
durch Wald und Flur,
über Fels und Stein,
sprachlos schweigend
sprangst du dahin;
kein Ruf hielt dich zur Rast.
(Sie starrt wild vor sich hin.)
Ruhe nun aus:
rede zu mir!
Ende des Schweigens Angst!
Sieh, dein Bruder
hält seine Braut:
Siegmund ist dir Gesell'!
(Er hat sie unvermerkt nach dem Steinsitze geleitet.)

SIEGLINDE
(blickt SIEGMUND mit wachsendem Entzücken in
die Augen; dann umschlingt sie leidenschaftlich seinen Hals. Endlich fährt sie mit jähem Schreck auf,
während SIEGMUND sie heftig fasst).

Hinweg! Hinweg!
flieh' die Entweihte!
Unheilig
umfängt dich ihr Arm;
entehrt, geschändet
schwand dieser Leib:
flieh' die Leiche,
lasse sie los!
der Wind mag sie verweh'n,
die ehrlos dem Edlen sich gab! — —
Da er sie liebend umfing,
da seligste Lust sie fand,
da ganz sie minnte der Mann,
der ganz ihr Minne geweckt —
vor der süssesten Wonne
heiligster Weihe,
die ganz ihr Sinn
und Seele durchdrang,
Grauen und Schauder
ob grässlichster Schande
musste mit Schreck
die Schmähliche fassen,
die je dem Manne gehorcht,
der ohne Minne sie hielt! —
Lass' die Verfluchte,
lass' sie dich flieh'n!
Verworfen bin ich,
der Würde bar!
Dir reinstem Manne
muss ich entrinnen;
dir herrlichem darf ich
nimmer gehören:
Schande bring' ich dem Bruder,
Schmach dem freienden Freund!

Whom in holy honor
Thy heart has long cherished—
Foe to him makes me never
Thy double-edg'd word.

WOTAN.

Ha! Brazen maid,
Bravest thou me?
What art thou, if not the willing,
Blind tool of my power?
When I gave thee being
Sank I so low
That my own creation
Can mock me to scorn?
Dread'st not, daughter, my wrath?
Less hardy thou wert
If e'er its flashes
Should seek thee to destroy!
Within my bosom
Rages such wrath
As would wreck and lay
Waste a whole world,
That once my heart did delight!
Woe to him whom it strikes!
Long his rashness he'd rue!—
So take thou heed
Rouse not my wrath;
But do what Wotan doth bid:—
Slay thou Siegmund!—
That be the Walkyrie's work.

(He hurries away and vanishes in the mountains to
the left.)

BRÜNNHILDE.

(Stands for some time as if stunned and terrified.)
So—Wotan
Ne'er did I see,
Though swiftly his wrongs he'd resent!
(She stoops mournfully and picks up her weapons,
with which she again arms herself.)
Down weighs me
My weapons' weight:—
Yet how light they seemed
When willingly borne!—
With heavy heart
Shall I fight to-day!
(She ponders and sighs.)
Woe! My Wälsung!
In sorest need
Must I falsely the faithful abandon!

(She moves towards the background and sees Siegmund and Sieglinde as they ascend from the ravine.
She watches them for a moment and then re-enters
the cave in which she has left her steed, so that she
is quite hidden from the spectators.)

(Siegmund and Sieglinde enter. She advances hastily. He tries to stop her.)

SIEGMUND.

Rest thou awhile:
Here there is peace!

SIEGLINDE.

Onward! Onward!

SIEGMUND.

(Putting his arm round her, firmly but tenderly.)
No further now!
Ah, stay, thou sweetest of wives!—
Thou'st run from our rapture,
Run from our joy,
With rushing haste,
Torn thyself free;
Scarce could I with thee keep pace:
Through wood and plain,
Over rock and hill,
Speechless, silent,
Fled'st thou away;
My call checked not thy flight.
(She stares wildly into vacancy.)
Rest thee now, sweet:
Speak but one word,
Ending this dumb dismay!
See, thy brother
Clings to his bride:
Siegmund now is thy mate!
(Meanwhile he has quietly led her to a rocky seat.)

SIEGLINDE.

(Looks at Siegmund with growing rapture and throws
her arms passionately round his neck. Then she sud-
denly starts up in terror, while Siegmund tries to
hold her.)
Away! Away!
Shun my dishonor!
Unholy's
The clasp of my arms:
Defiled, dishonored,
Let me be dead:
Flee this body,
Leave me, I'm lost!
O winds, sweep ye her hence
Who basely the hero beguiled!— —
Because he held her so dear,
And filled her with rapture rare,
Till all her heart was the man's,
Whose love her heart did awake!
In her joy—in her sweetest,
Holiest bliss, as
Her soul and sense
In passion were drowned,
Sudden a shudder
Of shame and of terror
Came with a shock
To shatter the sinner
Who once a husband had known
Unloved, unloving, and bound!—
Leave her, accursèd,
Leave her to flee!
An outcast am I,
Of honor shorn!
Thy purer passion
Must be denied me;
Thy bride, o my dear one,
Ne'er shouldst thou name me:
Shame I'd bring to the brother,
Scorn and woe to the friend!

SIEGMUND.

Was je Schande dir schuf,
das büsst nun des Frevlers Blut!
Drum fliehe nicht weiter;
harre des Feindes;
hier — soll er mir fallen:
wenn Nothung ihm
das Herz zernagt.
Rache dann hast du erreicht.

SIEGLINDE
(schrickt auf und lauscht).

Horch! die Hörner —
hörst du den Ruf? —
Ringsher tönt
wüthend Getös';
aus Wald und Gau
gellt es herauf.
Hunding erwachte
aus hartem Schlaf;
Sippen und Hunde
ruft er zusammen:
muthig gehetzt
heult die Meute,
wild bellt sie zum Himmel
um der Ehe gebrochenen Eid!
(Sie lacht wie wahnsinnig auf: — dann schrickt sie
ängstlich zusammen.)
Wo bist du, Siegmund?
seh' ich dich noch?
brünstig geliebter
leuchtender Bruder!
Deines Auges Stern
lass' noch einmal mir strahlen:
wehre dem Kuss
des verworf'nen Weibes nicht! —
Horch! o horch!
das ist Hunding's Horn!
Seine Meute naht
mit mächt'ger Wehr.
Kein Schwert frommt
vor der Hunde Schwall: —
wirf es fort, Siegmund! —
Siegmund — wo bist du? —
Ha dort — ich sehe dich —
schrecklich Gesicht! —
Rüden fletschen
die Zähne nach Fleisch;
sie achten nicht
deines edlen Blick's;
bei den Füssen packt dich
das feste Gebiss —
du fällst —
in Stücken zerstaucht das Schwert: —
die Esche stürzt —
es bricht der Stamm! —
Bruder! mein Bruder!
Siegmund! — ha! —
(Sie sinkt mit einem Schrei ohnmächtig in SIEG-
MUND'S Arme.)

SIEGMUND.

Schwester! Geliebte!
(Er lauscht ihrem Athem und überzeugt sich, dass
sie noch lebe. Er lässt sie an sich herabgleiten, so
dass sie, als er sich selbst zum Sitze niederlässt, mit
ihrem Haupt auf seinem Schooss zu ruhen kommt. In
dieser Stellung verbleiben beide bis zum Schlusse des
folgenden Auftrittes.
Langes Schweigen, während dessen SIEGMUND
mit zärtlicher Sorge über SIEGLINDE sich hinneigt,
und mit einem langen Kusse ihr die Stirn küsst. —
BRUENNHILDE ist, ihr Ross am Zaume geleitend
aus der Höhle langsam und feierlich nach vornen ge-
schritten und hält nun, SIEGMUND zur Seite, in
geringer Entfernung von ihm. Sie trägt Schild und
Speer in der einen Hand, lehnt sich mit der andren
an den Hals des Rosses und betrachtet so, in ernstem
Schweigen, eine Zeit lang SIEGMUND.)

BRUENNHILDE.

Siegmund —
Sieh' auf mich!
Ich — bin's,
der bald du folgst.

SIEGMUND
richtet den Blick zu ihr auf).

Wer bist du, sag',
die so schön und ernst mir erscheint?

BRUENNHILDE.

Nur Todgeweihten
taugt mein Anblick:
wer mich erschaut,
der scheidet vom Lebens-Licht.
Auf der Walstatt allein
erschein' ich Edlen:
wer mich gewahrt,
zur Wal kor ich ihn mir.

SIEGMUND
(blickt ihr lange in das Auge, senkt dann sinnend das
Haupt und wendet sich endlich mit feierlichem Ernste
wieder zu ihr).

Der dir nun folgt,
wohin führst du den Helden?

BRUENNHILDE.

Zu Walvater,
der dich gewählt,
führ' ich dich:
nach Walhall folgst du mir.

SIEGMUND.

In Walhall's Saal
Walvater find' ich allein?

BRUENNHILDE.

Gefall'ner Helden
hehre Schaar
umfängt dich hold
mit hoch-heiligem Gruss.

SIEGMUND.

Fänd' ich in Walhall
Wälse, den eig'nen Vater?

BRUENNHILDE.

Den Vater findet
der Wälsung dort.

SIEGMUND.

For the shame thou hast seen,
The blood of thy foe shall pay!
So flee thou no further;
Wait for his coming;
Here—surely I'll slay him:
When Nothung once
His heart shall gnaw,
Vengeance shall surely be thine!

SIEGLINDE.

(Starts up and listens.)

Hark! He calls thee!—
Hear'st thou the horns?—
Round and round
Fiercely they blare;
Through wood and vale
Wilder they ring.
Hunding has 'wakened,
No more he sleeps;
Kinsmen and bloodhounds
Come as he calls them:
Maddened with hate
Come the hunters,
Howl loudly to heaven
To avenge the offence to one wed!
(She laughs wildly, and then shudders.)
Where art thou, Siegmund?
Art thou still here?
Hotly belovèd
Beacon and brother!
Shall thy starlit eyes
Never more, then, delight me?
Spurn not the kiss
Of the outcast one, thy bride!—
Hark! o hark!
That is Hunding's horn!
And his host draws near
With hateful might.
No sword serves
Where yon hounds give tongue:—
Cast it d wn, Siegmund!—
Siegmund—where art thou?—
Ah, look!—I see thee there—
Dreadful the sight!—
Dogs are gnashing
Their ravening fangs;
No heed they pay
To thy fiery glance;
Now thy feet they seize in
Their pitiless maws—
Thou fall'st!—
In splinters now lies thy sword:—
The ash—it falls!—
The trunk is riv'n!
Brother! o brother!
Siegmund!—Ah!
(She gives a shriek and falls senseless into SIEG-
MUND'S arms.)

SIEGMUND.

Sister! Beloved!

(He listens to her breathing, and convinces himself
that she still lives. He lowers her gently, seats himself, and rests her head on his knee. In this position
they remain till the end of the next scene.

A long pause follows, while SIEGMUND bends tenderly over SIEGLINDE, and impresses a long kiss on her
brow.

Meanwhile BRÜNNHILDE, leading her steed by the
bridle, enters slowly from the cave and advances
solemnly. On nearing SIEGMUND, she halts. In one
hand she holds her shield and spear. With the other
she caresses the neck of her steed. For some time
she remains in this attitude, silently and earnestly
observing SIEGMUND.)

BRÜNNHILDE.

Siegmund—
Look on me!
I—wait.
Thine hour draws near.

SIEGMUND.

(Looking at her.)

Who art thou?—speak.
Thou art fair, though stern thou dost
    seem.

BRÜNNHILDE.

The doomed, they only
Know my glances:
Who me beholds
Must part with the light of life.
On the death-field alone
I come to heroes:
Him whom I meet,
To death bear I away.

SIEGMUND.

(Looks at her fixedly, bends his head as if reflecting,
and turns solemnly to her again.)

When thou dost call,
To what goal ride the heroes?

BRÜNNHILDE.

The War-Father,
Who thee did choose,
Waits for thee:
To Walhall ride we twain.

SIEGMUND.

In Walhall's hall
Liveth the War-Lord alone?

BRÜNNHILDE.

Of fallen heroes
Mighty hosts
Shall throng to greet thee,
And bid thee all-hail.

SIEGMUND.

Lives there in Walhall
Wälse, my own dear father?

BRÜNNHILDE.

The Wälsung's father
Shall there be found.

SIEGMUND.
Grüsst mich in Walhall
froh eine Frau?

BRUENNHILDE.
Wunschmädchen
walten dort hehr:
Wotan's Tochter
reicht dir traulich den Trank.

SIEGMUND.
Hehr bist du:
und heilig gewahr' ich
das Wotanskind:
doch Eines sag' mir, du Ew'ge!
Begleitet den Bruder
die bräutliche Schwester?
umfängt Siegmund
Sieglinde dort?

BRUENNHILDE.
Erdenluft
muss sie noch athmen:
Sieglinde
sieht Siegmund dort nicht!

SIEGMUND.
So grüsse mir Walhall,
grüsse mir Wotan,
grüsse mir Wälse
und alle Helden —
grüss' auch die holden
Wunsches-Mädchen:
zu ihnen folg' ich dir nicht.

BRUENNHILDE.
Du sahest der Walküre
sehrenden Blick:
mit ihr musst du nun zieh'n!

SIEGMUND.
Wo Sieglinde lebt
in Lust und Leid,
da will Siegmund auch säumen:
noch machte dein Blick
nicht mich erbleichen:
vom Bleiben zwingt er mich nie!

BRUENNHILDE.
So lang' du lebst
zwäng' dich wohl nichts;
doch zwingt dich Thoren der Tod: —
ihn dir zu künden
kam ich her.

SIEGMUND.
Wo wäre der Held,
dem heut' ich fiel?

BRUENNHILDE.
Hunding fällt dich im Streit.

SIEGMUND.
Mit stärk'rem drohe
als Hunding's Streichen!
Lauerst du hier

lüstern auf Wal.
jenen kiese zum Fang:
ich denk' ihn zu fällen im Kampf

BRUENNHILDE
(den Kopf schüttelnd).
Dir, Wälsung —
höre mich wohl! —
dir ward das Loos gekies't.

SIEGMUND.
Kennst du dies Schwert?
Der mir es schuf,
beschied mir Sieg:
deinem Drohen trotz' ich mit ihm!

BRUENNHILDE
(mit stark erhobener Stimme).
Der dir es schuf,
beschied dir jetzt Tod:
seine Tugend nimmt er dem Schwert!

SIEGMUND
(heftig).
Schweig' und schrecke
die Schlummernde nicht! —
(Er beugt sich, mit hervorbrechendem Schmerz
zärtlich über SIEGLINDE.)
Weh! Weh!
süssestes Weib!
Du traurigste aller Getreuen!
Gegen dich wüthet
in Waffen die Welt:
und ich, dem du einzig vertraut,
für den du ihr einzig getrotzt —
mit meinem Schutz
nicht soll ich dich schirmen,
die Kühne verrathen im Kampf?
O Schande ihm,
der das Schwert mir schuf,
beschied er mir Schimpf für Sieg!
Muss ich denn fallen,
nicht fahr' ich nach Walhall —
Hella halte mich fest!

BRUENNHILDE
(erschüttert).
So wenig achtest du
ewige Wonne?
Alles wär' dir
das arme Weib,
das müd' und harmvoll
matt auf dem Schoosse dir hängt?
Nichts sonst hieltest du hehr?

SIEGMUND
(bitter zu ihr aufblickend).
So jung und schön
erschimmerst du mir:
doch wie kalt und hart

SIEGMUND.
Shall no sweet woman
Wait in the hall?

BRÜNNHILDE.
Dream-maidens
Many are there:
Wotan's daughter
There thy beaker shall fill.

SIEGMUND.
High art thou,
And holy I know thee,
O Wotan's child.
Yet one thing tell me, thou goddess!
Shall she who is sister
Be bride to the brother?
Shall I, Siegmund,
Sieglinde woo?

BRÜNNHILDE.
Earthly air
Here she'll be breathing:
Sieglinde
Shall Siegmund not see!

SIEGMUND.
Then greet for me Walhall,
Greet for me Wotan,
Greet for me Wälse
And all the heroes—
Greet thou the blessèd
Beauteous maidens:
To them I go not with thee!

BRÜNNHILDE.
Thou'st seen the Walkyrie's
Withering glance:
Thou need'st must when she bids!

SIEGMUND.
Where Sieglinde lives
In joy or pain,
There will Siegmund still linger:
Thy look hath not chill'd
My heart with terror:
It shall not tear us apart!

BRÜNNHILDE.
While life shall last,
Hast thou thy way;
But yield thou must to dark Death:—
To hail his coming,
Came I here.

SIEGMUND.
Then whose is the hand
Shall lay me low?

BRÜNNHILDE.
Hunding's prey thou shalt be.

SIEGMUND.
I scorn the menace
Of Hunding's malice!
Lurk an thou wilt
Lusting for death:
Take thou him for thy prey—
Methinks I shall slay him to-day.

BRÜNNHILDE.
(Shaking her head.)
No, Wälsung!—
Heed thou my voice!—
Thou hast been doomed to die!

SIEGMUND.
Know'st thou this sword?
He who it wrought
Shall make me win:
With this steel thy threats I can brave!

BRÜNNHILDE.
(Raising her voice.)
He who it wrought
Now dooms thee to death:
For the sword he robs of its spell!

SIEGMUND.
(Angered.)
Peace! Disturb not
My slumbering bride!
(He bends tenderly and with anguish over SIEGLINDE.)
Woe! Woe!
Sweetest of wives!
Thou saddest of women, and truest
Round thee now
Rages in arms a whole world:
And I, whom alone thou didst trust,
For whom thou the world hast forsworn,
I may not shield
Nor serve thee, as shelter?
The brave am I doomed to betray?
O shame on him
Who the sword once wrought,
And makes me a mark for scorn!
Should I be vanquish'd,
I ride not to Walhall—
Hella's prey I will be!

BRÜNNHILDE.
(Agitated.)
So careless art thou
Of heavenly rapture?
One weak woman
To thee is all,
Who, worn and weary,
Hangs on thy knee for her rest!
Naught else holdest thou dear?

SIEGMUND.
(Looking up at her bitterly.)
So young and fair
On me thou dost shine:
Yet so cold and hard

kennt dich mein Herz! —
Kannst du nur höhnen,
so hebe dich fort,
du arge, fühllose Maid!
doch musst du dich weiden
an meinem Weh',
mein Leiden letze dich denn;
meine Noth labe
dein neidvolles Herz: —
nur von Walhall's spröden Wonnen
sprich du wahrlich mir nicht!

BRUENNHILDE
(mit wachsender Ergriffenheit).
Ich sehe die Noth,
die das Herz dir zernagt;
ich fühle des Helden
heiligen Harm — —
Siegmund, befiehl mir dein Weib;
mein Schutz umfange sie fest!

SIEGMUND.
Kein andrer als ich
soll die Reine lebend berühren:
verfiel ich dem Tod,
die Betäubte tödt' ich zuvor!

BRUENNHILDE.
Wälsung! Rasender!
Hör' meinen Rath:
befiehl mir dein Weib
um des Pfandes willen,
das wonnig von dir es empfing!

SIEGMUND
(sein Schwert ziehend).
diess Schwert —
das dem Treuen ein Trugvoller schuf;
diess Schwert —
das feig vor dem Feind mich verräth: —
frommt es nicht gegen den Feind,
so fromm' es denn wider den Freund! —
(Das Schwert auf SIEGLINDE zückend.)
Zwei Leben
lachen dir hier: —
nimm sie, Nothung,
neidischer Stahl!
nimm sie mit einem Streich!

BRUENNHILDE
(im heftigsten Sturme des Mitgefühls).
Halt' ein, Wälsung!
höre mein Wort!
Sieglinde lebe —
und Siegmund lebe mit ihr!
Beschlossen ist's;
das Schlachtloos wend' ich;
dir, Siegmund,
schaff' ich Segen und Sieg!
(Man hört aus dem fernen Hintergrunde Hornrufe
erschallen.)
Hörst du den Ruf?
Nun rüste dich, Held!

Traue dem Schwert
und schwing' es getrost:
treu hält dir die Wehr,
wie die Walküre treu dich schützt! —
Leb' wohl, Siegmund,
seligster Held!
auf der Walstatt grüss' ich dich wiede
(Sie stürmt fort und verschwindet mit dem Ro
rechts in einer Seitenschlucht. SIEGMUND bli
ihr freudig und erhoben nach.
Die Bühne hat sich allmälig verfinstert; schw
Gewitterwolken senken sich auf den Hintergru
herab und hüllen die Gebirgswände, die Schlucht u
das erhöhte Bergjoch nach und nach gänzlich ein.
Von allen Seiten lassen sich aus der Ferne Rufe v
Heerhörnern vernehmen, die während des Folgend
allmälig näher erschallen.)

SIEGMUND
(über SIEGLINDE sich beugend).
Zauberfest
bezähmt ein Schlaf
der Holden Schmerz und Harm:
da die Walküre zu mir trat,
schuf sie ihr den wonnigen Trost?
Sollte die grimmige Wal
nicht schrecken ein gramvolles Weib?
Leblos scheint sie,
die dennoch lebt:
der Traurigen kos't
ein lächelnder Traum. —
(Neue Hornrufe.)
So schlumm're nun fort,
bis die Schlacht gekämpft,
und Friede dich erfreu'!
(Er legt sich sanft auf den Steinsitz, küsst ihr d
Stirn und bricht dann, nach abermaligen Hornrufe
auf.)
Der dort mich ruft,
rüste dich nun;
was ihm gebührt,
biet' ich ihm:
Nothung zahl' ihm den Zoll!
(Er eilt dem Hintergrunde zu, und verschwindet a
dem Joche sogleich in finstres Gewittergewölk.)

SIEGLINDE
(träumend).
Kehrte der Vater nun heim!
Mit dem Knaben noch weilt er im Forst
Mutter! Mutter!
mir bangt der Muth: —
nicht freund und friedlich
scheinen die Fremden! —
Schwarze Dämpfe —
schwüles Gedünst —
feurige Lohe
leckt schon nach uns —
es brennt das Haus —
zu Hülfe, Bruder!
Siegmund! Siegmund!
(Starke Blitze zucken durch das Gewölk auf; ei
furchtbarer Donnerschlag erweckt SIEGLINDE: si
springt jäh auf.)

Siegmund! — Ha!
(Sie starrt mit steigender Angst um sich her; — fas
die ganze Bühne ist in schwarze Gewitterwolken ver
hüllt; fortwährender Blitz und Donner. Von alle
Seiten dringen immer näher Hornrufe her.)

Now knows thee my heart!—
Must thou go mocking,
Most cruel of maids?
Then go and leave me alone!
But when thou hast sated
Thyself with woe,
On sorrow feasted thine eyes;
Though thy heart glow at
The sight of my pain:—
When thou paintest Walhall's pleasures,
All thy pleading thou'lt waste!

BRÜNNHILDE.
(With growing emotion.)
The pain I behold
That thy heart doth weigh down;
I feel all the hero's
Woe and dismay
Siegmund, trust me with thy wife;
My shield her shelter shall be!

SIEGMUND.
No being but I,
While she lives, shall dare to approach
her:
And though I be doom'd,
Ere she awake, my bride I will slay!

BRÜNNHILDE.
Wälsung! Reckless one!
Heed but my rede!
Entrust her to me,
For a pledge she brings thee
Of rapture and love thou hast giv'n!

SIEGMUND.
(Drawing his sword.)
This sword—
That a traitor erst wrought for one true;
This sword—
That soon shall its master undo:
Faithless when fronting the foe,
Shall faithfully strike at the friend!
(Turning the sword against SIEGLINDE.)
Two lives lie
Here at thy call:—
Take them, Nothung,
Traitorous steel!
Take them at one fell stroke!

BRÜNNHILDE.
(Stirred to the depths by sympathy.)
Forbear, Wälsung!
Hear thou my words!
Life to Sieglinde—
And life to Siegmund I bring!
'Tis sworn and done;
Thy sword shall conquer:
Thou, Siegmund,
Victor soon shalt be hailed!
(The faint sound of horns is heard in the background.)
Dost hear the call?
Now, hero, to arms!

Trust to thy sword
And wield it right well:
True still be thy blade,
As the Walkyr, thy true, sure shield!—
Farewell, Siegmund,
Bravest of all!
On the field will I give thee greeting!
(She rushes off with her steed, by way of a ravine on
the right. SIEGMUND follows her with his eyes, and
seems elated with joy. The stage, meanwhile, has
gradually grown dark. Heavy thunderclouds have
descended in the background, hiding the hills, the
ravine and the lofty rocks in the foreground. Distant
sounds of horns are heard on all sides, and continue
to be heard throughout the following scene. Gradually
they grow louder.)

SIEGMUND.
(Bending over SIEGLINDE.)
Locked in sleep,
Her lovely eyes
To pain and woe are blind.
Did the Walkyr, with magic art,
Bring her this most merciful rest?
Was the wild fury of war
Not fated her heart to affright?
Lifeless seeming,
She clings to life:
Her sorrow is still'd,
And smiling she dreams.—
Then slumber in peace,
Till the strife is o'er,
And peril all is past!
(He lays her gently on the rocky seat, kisses her on
the brow, and, after the horns have again been heard,
makes ready to go.)
Let him who calls
Arm for the fight;
What he demands
Soon he'll find:
Nothung now he shall know!
(He hurries towards the background and disappears
beyond the rocky arch, which is instantly hidden by
dark thunderclouds.)

SIEGLINDE.
(Dreaming.)
Would that my father were home?
With his boy he still roams in the woods.
Mother! Mother!
I'm filled with dread:—
How stern and solemn
Seem all these strangers!—
Smoke and darkness—
Sulphurous fumes—
Roaring and leaping,
Follow the flames—
The house—it burns—
O help me, brother!
Siegmund! Siegmund!
(Vivid lightnings flash from the clouds. A terrible
thunderbolt wakes SIEGLINDE. She leaps to her feet
in alarm.)

Siegmund! Ah!
(She stares in all directions with growing terror. The
stage is almost entirely wrapped in dark clouds. Thunder and lightning. Horns are heard calling on all
sides, and growing louder.)

HUNDING'S
(Stimme im Hintergrunde, vom Bergjoche her).

Wehwalt! Wehwalt!
Steh' mir zum Streit,
sollen dich Hunde nicht halten!

SIEGMUND'S
(Stimme, von weiter hinten her, aus der Schlucht).

Wo birgst du dich,
dass ich vorbei dir schoss?
Steh' dort, dass ich dich stelle!

SIEGLINDE
(die in furchtbarer Aufregung lauscht).

Hunding — Siegmund —
könnt' ich sie sehen!

HUNDING'S
(Stimme).

Hieher, du frevelnder Freier:
Fricka fälle dich hier!

SIEGMUND'S
(Stimme, nun ebenfalls auf dem Bergjoche).

Noch wähnst du mich waffenlos,
feiger Wicht?
Drohst du mit Frauen,
so ficht nun selber,
sonst lässt dich Fricka im Stich!
Denn sieh': deines Hauses
heimischem Stamm
entzog ich zaglos das Schwert;
seine Schneide schmecke jetzt du!

(Ein Blitz erhellt für einen Augenblick den Bergjoch, auf welchem jetzt HUNDING und SIEGMUND kämpfend gewahrt worden.)

SIEGLINDE
(mit höchster Kraft).

Haltet ein, ihr Männer,
mordet erst mich!

(Sie stürzt auf das Bergjoch zu: ein von rechts her über die Kämpfer ausbrechender heller Schein blendet sie aber plötzlich so heftig, dass sie wie erblindet zur Seite schwankt. In dem Lichtglanze erscheint BRUENNHILDE über SIEGMUND schwebend und diesen mit dem Schilde deckend.)

BRUENNHILDE'S
(Stimme).

Triff' ihn, Siegmund!
Traue dem Schwert!

(Als SIEGMUND so eben zu einem tödtlichen Streiche auf HUNDING ausholt, bricht von links her ein glühend röthlicher Schein durch das Gewölk aus, in welchem WOTAN erscheint, über HUNDING stehend und seinen Speer SIEGMUND quer entgegenhaltend.)

WOTAN'S
(Stimme).

Zurück vor dem Speer!
In Stücken das Schwert!

(BRUENNHILDE ist vor Wotan mit dem Schilde erschrocken zurückgewichen: SIEGMUND'S Schwert zerspringt an dem vorgestreckten Speere; dem Unbewehrten stösst HUNDING sein Schwert in die Brust. SIEGMUND stürzt zu Boden. — SIEGLINDE, die seinen Todesseufzer gehört, sinkt mit einem Schrei, wie leblos zusammen.
Mit SIEGMUND'S Fall ist zugleich von beiden Seiten der glänzende Schein verschwunden; dichte Finsterniss ruht im Gewölk bis nach vorn; in ihm wird BRUENNHILDE undeutlich sichtbar, wie sie in jäher Hast SIEGLINDEN sich zugewendet.)

BRUENNHILDE.

Zu Ross, dass ich dich rette!

(Sie hebt SIEGLINDE schnell zu sich auf ihr, der Seitenschlucht nahe stehendes Ross und verschwindet sogleich gänzlich mit ihr.
Alsbald zertheilt sich das Gewölk in der Mitte, so dass man deutlich HUNDING gewahrt, wie er sein Schwert dem gefallenen SIEGMUND aus der Brust zieht. — WOTAN, von Gewölk umgeben, steht hinter ihm auf einem Felsen, an seinen Speer gelehnt und schmerzlich auf SIEGMUND'S Leiche blickend.)

WOTAN
(nach einem kleinen Schweigen, zu HUNDING gewandt).

Geh' hin, Knecht!
Kniee vor Fricka:
meld' ihr, dass Wotan's Speer
gerächt, was Spott ihr schuf. —
Geh'! — Geh'! —

(Vor seinem verächtlichen Handwink sinkt HUNDING todt zu Boden.)

WOTAN
(plötzlich in furchtbarer Wuth auffahrend).

Doch Brünnhilde —
weh' der Verbrecherin!
Furchtbar sei
die Freche gestraft,
erreicht mein Ross ihre Flucht!

(Er verschwindet mit Blitz und Donner. — Der Vorhang fällt schnell.)

DRITTER AUFZUG.

Auf dem Gipfel eines Felsberges.

Rechts begrenzt ein Tannenwald die Scene. Links der Eingang einer Felshöhle, die einen natürlichen Saal bildet: darüber steigt der Fels zu seiner höchsten Spitze auf. Nach hinten ist die Aussicht gänzlich frei; höhere und niedere Felssteine bilden den Rand vor dem Abhange, der — wie anzunehmen ist — nach dem Hintergrunde zu steil hinabführt. — Einzelne Wolkenzüge jagen, wie vom Sturm getrieben, am Felsensaume vorbei.

(Die Namen der acht Walküren, welche — ausser BRUENNHILDE — in dieser Scene auftreten, sind: GERHILDE, ORTLINDE, WALTRAUTE, SCHWERTLEITE, HELMWIGE, SIEGRUNE, GRIMGERDE, ROSSWEISSE.)
GERHILDE, ORTLINDE, WALTRAUTE und SCHWERTLEITE haben sich auf der Felsspitze, an und über der Höhle, gelagert; sie sind in voller Waffenrüstung.

GERHILDE
(zu höchst gelagert und dem Hintergrunde zugewendet).

Hojotoho! Hojotoho!
Heiaha! Heiaha!
Helmwige, hier!
Hieher mit dem Ross!

(In einem vorbeiziehenden Gewölk bricht Blitzesglanz aus; eine Walküre zu Ross wird in ihm sichtbar; über ihrem Sattel hängt ein erschlagener Krieger.)

HELMWIGE'S
(Stimme, von aussen).

Hojotoho! Hojotoho!
Hojotoho! Hojotoho!

GERHILDE, WALTRAUTE und

SCHWERTLEITE
(der Ankommenden entgegenrufend).

Heiaha!

(Die Wolke mit der Erscheinung ist rechts hinter dem Tann verschwunden.)

ORTLINDE
(in den Tann hineinrufend).

Zu Ortlinde's Stute
stell' deinen Hengst:

HUNDING'S VOICE.

(Heard from the rocky arch in the background.)
Woeful! Woeful!
Stand and give fight—
e where the hounds would devour thee!

SIEGMUND'S VOICE.

(Heard more in the distance from the ravine.)
Where hidest thou?
How did I miss thee, hound?
Stand, let me but face thee!

SIEGLINDE.

(Listening, horror struck.)
Hunding—Siegmund—
Could I but see them!

HUNDING'S VOICE.

This way, thou lecherous lover:
Fricka waits for thee here!

SIEGMUND'S VOICE.

(Now also heard from the rocky arch.)
Dost ween I am weaponless,
Craven wight?
Bold but with women—
Now fight thy fiercest,
Lest Fricka fail thee in need!
For see: from the ashen
Tree in thy home
Unstayed I stole my keen sword;
With its steel I'll slay thee to-day.

flash of lightning lights up the rocky arch for a
ment. HUNDING and SIEGMUND are seen fighting.)

SIEGLINDE.

(At the top of her voice.)
Hold your hands, ye foemen!
Murder me first!

he rushes toward the rocks, but stops, blinded by
sudden and terrific flash that comes from the right.
e totters. BRÜNNHILDE appears in the lightning,
vering about SIEGMUND and protecting him with
her shield.)

BRÜNNHILDE'S VOICE.

Slay him, Siegmund!
Trust in thy sword!

s SIEGMUND aims a deadly blow at HUNDING, a
ddish glow comes through the clouds at the left of
e rocks, heralding WOTAN, who stands above HUN-
DING and points his spear at SIEGMUND.)

WOTAN'S VOICE.

Back, back! from the spear!
Down, down! with thy sword!

RÜNNHILDE, with her shield has recoiled in terror,
the approach of WOTAN. SIEGMUND'S sword is
vered to pieces against the outstretched spear. HUN-
NG thrusts his sword into the breast of his defence-
s foe. SIEGMUND falls. SIEGLINDE, who has heard
his dying groan, shrieks and falls senseless.)
s SIEGMUND falls, the glow vanishes and the light-
ng stops. Darkness enshrouds the scene. BRÜNN-
LDE is dimly visible as she hastens to the assistance of SIEGLINDE.)

BRÜNNHILDE.

To horse! and I will save thee!

(She lifts SIEGLINDE swiftly into the saddle as she
hurries to her horse in the cave on the right, and
both disappear.)
(Instantly the clouds roll back on either side, plainly disclosing HUNDING, as he draws his sword from
the breast of SIEGMUND. WOTAN, surrounded by
clouds, stands behind him on a rock, leaning against
his spear, and gazing sorrowfully on SIEGMUND's
body.)

WOTAN.

(Turning to HUNDING, after a brief pause.)
Away, slave!
Kneel thou to Fricka:
Tell her that Wotan's spear
Avenged what brought her shame.—
Go!—Go!—

(At a contemptuous gesture of WOTAN's hand, HUN-
DING falls dead.)

WOTAN.

(Breaking suddenly into a fury of wrath.)
But Brünnhilde—
Woe to who braveth me!
Dread shall be
The fate she must know,
For Wotan rides in her wake!

(He vanishes amid thunder and lightning. Quick
curtain.)

ACT THREE.

The Summit of a Rocky Hill.

To the right is a forest of fir-trees. To the left is
the entrance to a cave which forms a natural hall.
Above it rises the highest of the peaks. At the back,
the view is uninterrupted. Rocks of various sizes form
an embankment of the supposed precipice in the rear.
Detached clouds, storm-swept, drift swiftly past the
peak.
The names of the eight Walkyrs, exclusive of
BRÜNNHILDE, who appear, are: GERHILDE, ORTLINDE,
WALTRAUTE, SCHWERTLEITE, HELMWIGE, SIEGRUNE,
GRIMGERDE, and ROSSWEISSE.
GERHILDE, ORTLINDE, WALTRAUTE and SCHWERTLEITE
are stationed on the peak near and above the cave.
They are in full armor.

GERHILDE.

(At the summit of the peak, with her face towards
the back.)
Ho-yo-to ho! Ho-yo-to-ho!
Hi-ya-ha! Hi-ya-ha!
Helmwige, here!
Hie here on thy horse!

(Lightning flashes from one of the clouds that drift
by, revealing a mounted Walkyr. From her saddle-
bow hangs a warrior, slain in fight.)

HELMWIGE'S VOICE.

(Without.)
Ho-yo-to-ho! Ho-yo-to-ho!
Ho-yo-to-ho! Ho-yo-to-ho!
Hi-ya-ha!

GERHILDE, WALTRAUTE and SCHWERTLEITE.

(Calling to the newcomer.)
Hi-ya-ha! Hi-ya-ha!

(The cloud with the apparition has disappeared behind a fir-tree on the right.)

ORTLINDE.

(Shouting in the direction of the fir-tree.)
In Ortlinde's stable
Tether thy steed:

mit meiner Grauen
gras't gern dein Brauner!

WALTRAUTE
(ebenso).
Wer hängt dir im Sattel?

HELMWIGE
(aus dem Tann schreitend).
Sintolt der Hegeling!

SCHWERTLEITE.
Führ' deinen Braunen
fort von der Grauen:
Ortlinde's Mähre
trägt Wittig, den Irming!

GERHILDE
(ist etwas näher herabgestiegen).
Als Feinde nur sah ich
Sintolt und Wittig.

ORTLINDE
(bricht schnell auf und läuft in den Tann).
Heiaha! Heiaha! Die Stute
stösst mir der Hengst!

SCHWERTLEITE und GERHILDE
(lachen laut auf).
Der Recken Zwist
entzweit noch die Rosse!

HELMWIGE
(in den Tann zurückrufend).
Ruhig dort, Brauner!
Brich nicht den Frieden!

WALTRAUTE
(hat für GERHILDE die Wacht auf der äussersten
Spitze genommen).
Hojoho! Hojoho!
Siegrune, hier!
Wo säumst du so lang?
(Wie zuvor HELMWIGE, zieht jetzt SIEGRUNE im
gleichen Aufzuge vorbei, dem Tann zu.)

SIEGRUNE'S
(Stimme von rechts).
Arbeit gab's!
Sind die And'ren schon da?

DIE WALKUEREN.
Hojotoho! Hojotoho!
Heiaha! Heiaha!
(SIEGRUNE ist hinter dem Tann verschwunden. Aus
der Tiefe hört man zwei Stimmen zugleich.)

GRIMGERDE und ROSSWEISSE
(von unten).
Hojotoho! Hojotoho!
Heiaha! Heiaha!

WALTRAUTE.
Rossweiss' und Grimgerde!

GERHILDE.
Sie reiten zu zwei.
(ORTLINDE ist mit HELMWIGE und der so eben
angekommenen SIEGRUNE aus dem Tann herausge-
treten: zu drei winken sie von dem hinteren Fels-
saume hinab.)

ORTLINDE, HELMWIGE und
SIEGRUNE.
Gegrüsst, ihr Reissige!
Rossweiss' und Grimgerde!

DIE ANDREN WALKUEREN
ALLE.
Hojotoho! Hojotoho!
Heiaha! Heiaha!
(In einem blitzerglänzenden Wolkenzuge, der von
ten heraufsteigt und dann hinter dem Tann v
schwindet, erschinen GRIMGERDE und ROS
WEISSE, ebenfalls auf Rossen, jede einen Erschla
nen im Sattel führend.)

GERHILDE.
In Wald mit den Rossen
zu Rast und Weid'!

ORTLINDE
(in den Tann rufend).
Führt die Mähren
fern von einander,
bis uns'rer Helden
Hass sich gelegt!

HELMWIGE.
(während die Andern lachen).
Der Helden Grimm
schon büsste die Graue!
(GRIMGERDE und ROSSWEISSE treten aus de
Tann auf.)

DIE WALKUEREN.
Willkommen! Willkommen!

SCHWERTLEITE.
War't ihr Kühnen zu zwei?

GRIMGERDE.
Getrennt ritten wir,
trafen uns heut'.

ROSSWEISSE.
Sind wir alle versammelt,
so säumt nicht lange:
nach Walhall brechen wir auf,
Wotan zu bringen die Wal.

HELMWIGE.
Acht sind wir erst,
eine noch fehlt.

GERHILDE.
Bei dem braunen Wälsung
weilt wohl noch Brünnhild'?

WALTRAUTE.
Auf sie noch harren
müssen wir hier:
Walvater gäb' uns
grimmigen Gruss,
säh' ohne sie er uns nah'n!

SIEGRUNE
(auf der Felsspitze, von wo sie hinausspäht).
Hojotoho! Hojotoho!
Hieher! Hieher!

With my grey mare
Thy bay were well mated!

WALTRAUTE.
(As above.)
Who hangs from thy saddle?

HELMWIGE.
(Issuing from behind the fir-tree.)
Sintolt, the Hegeling!

SCHWERTLEITE.
Stable thy charger
Not with Ortlinde's:
Wittig, the Irming,
Her mare has been bearing!

GERHILDE.
(Descending a few steps.)
And foes were they aye,
Your Sintolt and Wittig!

ORTLINDE.
(Suddenly darting over to the fir-tree.)
Hi-ya-ha! Hi-ya-ha!
My beauty's locked with thy bay!

SCHWERTLEITE AND GERHILDE.
(Laughing wildly.)
The heroes' wrongs
The horses remember!

HELMWIGE.
(Shouting back into the trees.)
Quiet, there, quiet!
Why would ye quarrel?

WALTRAUTE.
(Who has taken the place of GERHILDE at the top of
the peak.)
Ho-yo-ho! Ho-yo-ho!
Siegrune, here!
Why stayed thou so long?
(SIEGRUNE rides by, as HELMWIGE did, in the direction
of the fir-tree.)

SIEGRUNE'S VOICE.
(From the right.)
Work to do!
Are the rest of ye met?

THE WALKYRS.
Ho-yo-to-ho! Ho-yo-to-ho!
Hi-ya-ha! Hi-ya-ha!
(SIEGRUNE has disappeared behind the firs. Two voices
are heard together from the depths.)

GRIMGERDE and ROSSWEISSE.
(From below.)
Ho-yo-to-ho! Ho-yo-to-ho!
Hi-ya-ha! Hi-ya-ha!

WALTRAUTE.
Rossweiss' and Grimgerde!

GERHILDE.
They ride two by two.
ORTLINDE, with HELMWIGE and SIEGRUNE, has issued
om the firs. All three wave their hands from the
hindermost rocks.)

ORTLINDE, HELMWIGE and SIEGRUNE.
We greet thee, Rossweisse!
We greet thee, Grimgerde!

THE OTHER WALKYRS.
Ho-yo-to-ho! Ho-yo-to-ho!
Hi-ya-ha! Hi-ya-ha!
(GRIMGERDE and ROSSWEISSE, mounted, appear in a
glowing thundercloud which ascends from the depths
and vanishes behind the fir-tree. Each carries a slain
warrior at her saddle-bow.)

GERHILDE.
Away with the horses,
To feed and rest!

ORTLINDE.
(Shouting into the trees.)
Keep ye the chargers
Clear of each other,
Till all the heroes'
Hate is allayed!

HELMWIGE.
(Amid the laughter of her companions.)
The grey has paid
For their feuds and quarrels!
(GRIMGERDE and ROSSWEISSE issuing from the fir-trees.)

THE WALKYRS.
O welcome! O welcome!

SCHWERTLEITE.
Came ye single, or twain?

GRIMGERDE.
Alone galloped we,
And met on our way.

ROSSWEISSE.
If we all are assembled
No more we'll tarry:
To Walhall haste and away;
Wotan our coming awaits.

HELMWIGE.
Eight are we here.
One we still lack.

GERHILDE.
For the warrior Wälsung
Waiteth Brünnhilde.

WALTRAUTE.
Then till she cometh,
Here we must wait:
Grim were the greeting
Wotan would give,
Were she not there when we came!

SIEGRUNE.
(Peering into the distance from the top of the peak.)
Ho-yo-to-ho! Ho-yo-to-ho!
Hie here! Hie here!

In brünstigem Ritt
jagt Brünnhilde her.

DIE WALKUEREN
(nach der Felsspitze eilend).

Heiaha! Hojotoho! Hojotoho!
Brünnhilde! hei!

WALTRAUTE.

Nach dem Tann lenkt sie
das taumelnde Ross.

GRIMGERDE.

Wie schnaubt Grane
vom schnellen Ritt!

ROSSWEISSE.

So jach sah ich nie
Walküren jagen!

ORTLINDE.

Was hält sie im Sattel?

HELMWIGE.

Das ist kein Held!

SIEGRUNE.

Eine Frau führt sie.

GERHILDE.

Wie fand sie die Frau?

SCHWERTLEITE.

Mit keinem Gruss
grüsst sie die Schwestern?

WALTRAUTE.

Heiaha! Brünnhilde!
hörst du uns nicht?

ORTLINDE.

Helft der Schwester
vom Ross sich schwingen!

DIE WALKUEREN.

Hojotoho! Hojotoho!
Heiaha! Heiaha!
(GERHILDE und HELMWIGE stürzen in den
Tann.)

WALTRAUTE.

Zu Grunde stürzt
Grane der starke!
(SIEGRUNE und WALTRAUTE folgen den beiden.)

GRIMGERDE.

Aus dem Sattel hebt sie
hastig das Weib.

DIE UEBRIGEN WALKUEREN
(dem Tann zueilend).

Schwester! Schwester!
Was ist gescheh'n?
(Alle Walküren kehren auf die Bühne zu-
rück; mit ihnen kommt BRUENNHILDE, SIEG-
LINDE unterstützend und hereingeleitend.)

BRUENNHILDE
(athemlos).

Schützt mich, und helft
in höchster Noth!

DIE WALKUEREN.

Wo rittest du her
in rasender Hast?
So fliegt nur, wer auf der Flucht!

BRUENNHILDE.

Zum erstenmal flieh' ich
und bin verfolgt!
Heervater hetzt mir nach!

DIE WALKUEREN.
(heftig erschreckend).

Bist du von Sinnen?
Sage uns! Wie?
Verfolgt dich Heervater?
fliehst du vor ihm?

BRUENNHILDE
(ängstlich).

O Schwestern, späht
von des Felsens Spitze!
Schaut nach Norden,
ob Walvater naht!
(ORTLINDE und WALTRAUTE springen hinauf, um
zu spähen.)
Schnell! seht ihr ihn schon?

ORTLINDE.

Gewittersturm
naht von Norden.

WALTRAUTE.

Starkes Gewölk
staut sich dort auf.

DIE WALKUEREN.

Heervater reitet
sein heiliges Ross!

BRUENNHILDE.

Der wilde Jäger,
der wüthend mich jagt,
er naht, er naht von Nord!
Schützt mich, Schwestern!
wahret dies Weib!

DIE WALKUEREN.

Was ist mit dem Weibe?

BRUENNHILDE.

Hört mich in Eile!
Sieglinde ist es,
Siegmund's Schwester und Braut:
Gegen die Wälsungen
wüthet Wotan in Grimm: —
dem Bruder sollte
Brünnhilde heut'
entziehen den Sieg,
doch Siegmund schützt' ich
mit meinem Schild,

Brünnhilde comes riding
Madly this way!

THE WALKYRS.
(Hurrying to the summit.)
Ho-yo-to-ho! Ho-yo-to-ho!
Hi-ya-ha!
Brünnhilde! Heigh!

WALTRAUTE.
To the wood rushes
Her staggering steed.

GRIMGERDE.
See how Grane
Doth pant and strain!

ROSSWEISE.
So fast did I ne'er
See Walkyrs flying!

ORTLINDE.
What hangs at her saddle?

HELMWIGE.
That is no man!

SIEGRUNE.
'Tis a weak woman.

GERHILDE.
And where was she found?

SCHWERTLEITE.
No greeting glad
Gives she her sisters.

WALTRAUTE.
Hi-ya-ha! Brünnhilde!
Canst thou not hear?

ORTLINDE.
Help our sister
To leave the saddle!

THE WALKYRS.
Ho-yo-to-ho! Ho-yo-to-ho!
Hi-ya-ha! Hi-ya-ha!
(Gerhilde and Helmwige rush into the fir-trees.)

WALTRAUTE.
Now Grane groans,
Trembles and totters!
(Siegrune and Waltraute follow the two others.)

GRIMGERDE.
From the saddle, quick
The woman she lifts.

THE REMAINING WALKYRS.
(Hurrying towards the fir-trees.)
Sister! Sister!
What is thy pain?
(All the Walkyrs return. With them comes Brünn-
hilde, supporting and guiding Sieglinde.)

BRÜNNHILDE.
(Breathless.)
Shield me, and help
In direst need!

THE WALKYRS.
Whence ridest thou here
In furious haste?
So flieth but one who flees!

BRÜNNHILDE.
I flee, who fled never,
And fear pursuit!
Wotan has pressed me hard!

THE WALKYRS.
(In wild excitement.)
Hast thou thy senses?
Speak! Speak to us!
Does Wotan follow thee?
Fleest thou from him?

BRÜNNHILDE.
(Anxiously.)
O sisters, watch
From the rocky summit!
Look ye northward.
Is Wotan not near?
(Ortlinde and Waltraute rush to the summit and
look off.)
Quick! Comes he this way?

ORTLINDE.
A thunderstorm
Comes from northward.

WALTRAUTE.
Dark are the clouds,
Denser they grow.

THE WALKYRS.
Wotan comes riding
His terrible steed.

BRÜNNHILDE.
The dreadful hunter
Who's hunting me down,
Draws near from northward!
Shield me, sisters!
Shelter the waif!

THE WALKYRS.
What troubles this woman?

BRÜNNHILDE.
Haste ye and hear me!
Sieglinde is she,
Siegmund's sister and bride:
'Gainst the two Wälsungs was
Wotan's anger aroused:—
Brünnhilde bade be
Siegmund to-day
To doom to defeat.
But, braving Wotan,
I, with my shield,

trotzend dem Gott: —
der traf ihn da selbst mit dem Speer.
Siegmund fiel:
doch ich floh
fern mit der Frau:
sie zu retten
eilt' ich zu euch,
ob mich bange auch
ihr berget vor dem strafenden Streich.

DIE WALKUEREN.
(in grösster Bestürzung).
Bethörte Schwester!
Was thatest du?
Wehe! Wehe!
Brünnhilde, wehe!
Brach ungehorsam
Brünnhilde
Heervaters heilig Gebot?

WALTRAUTE
(von der Höhe).
Nächtig zieht es
von Norden heran.

ORTLINDE
(ebenso).
Wüthend steuert
hierher der Sturm.

SIEGRUNE.
(dem Hintergrunde zugewendet).
Wild wiehert
Walvaters Ross,
schrecklich schnaubt es daher!

BRUENNHILDE.
Wehe der Armen,
wenn Wotan sie trifft,
den Wälsungen allen
droht er Verderben! —
Wer leih't mir von euch
das leichteste Ross,
das flink die Frau ihm entführ'?

SIEGRUNE.
Auch uns räth'st du
rasenden Trotz?

BRUENNHILDE.
Rossweisse, Schwester!
Leih' mir deinen Renner!

ROSSWEISSE.
Vor Walvater floh
der fliegende nie.

BRUENNHILDE.
Helmwige, höre!

HELMWIGE.
Dem Vater gehorch' ich.

BRUENNHILDE.
Grimgerde! Gerhilde!
Gönnt mir eu'r Ross!
Schwertleite! Siegrune!
Seht meine Angst!
O seid mir treu,
wie traut ich euch war:
rettet diess traurige Weib!

SIEGLINDE
(die bisher finster und kalt vor sich hingestarrt, fährt
auf, als BRUENNHILDE sie lebhaft — wie zum
Schutze — umfasst).
Nicht sehre dich Sorge um mich:
einzig taugt mir der Tod!
Wer hiess dich Maid
dem Harst mich entführen?
Im Sturm dort hätt' ich
den Streich empfah'n
von derselben Waffe,
der Siegmund fiel:
das Ende fand ich
vereint mit ihm!
Fern von Siegmund —
Siegmund von dir!
O deckte mich Tod,
dass ich's denke! —
Soll um die Flucht
dir Maid ich nicht fluchen,
so erhöre heilig mein Fleh'n —
stosse dein Schwert mir in's Herz!

BRUENNHILDE.
Lebe, o Weib,
um der Liebe willen!
Rette das Pfand,
das von ihm du empfingst:
ein Wälsung wächst dir im Schooss.

SIEGLINDE
(ist heftig erschrocken; plötzlich strahlt dann das Gesicht in erhabener Freude auf).
Rette mich, Kühne!
rette mein Kind!
Schirmt mich, ihr Mädchen,
mit mächtigstem Schutz!
(Furchtbares Gewitter steigt im Hintergrunde auf;
nahender Donner.)

WALTRAUTE
(von der Höhe).
Der Sturm kommt heran.

ORTLINDE
(ebenso).
Flieh', wer ihn fürchtet!

DIE WALKUEREN.
Fort mit dem Weibe,
droht ihm Gefahr:
der Walküren keine
wag' ihren Schutz!

Siegmund did aid:—
Then slew him the god with his spear.
Siegmund fell:
But I fled
Far with his bride:
Now to save her
Hither I hied,
Though ye trembling give
Me shelter from the wrath that ye dread.

THE WALKYRS.
(In consternation.)
Misguided sister!
What didst thou then?
Woe's me!
Brünnhilde, woe's me!
Couldst thou, Brünnhilde,
Durst thou the War-father's
Will to defy?

WALTRAUTE.
(From the height.)
Dark and darker
To north it has grown.

ORTLINDE.
(As above.)
Rushing on
Comes the storm.

THE WALKYRS.
(Turning towards the background.)
Loud neigheth
Wotan's wild steed:
Snorting, panting, it comes!

BRÜNNHILDE.
Woe to this victim
When Wotan shall come!
For all of the Wälsungs
Vows he to ruin!—
Which one of ye all
Will lend me a steed
To rob the god of his prey?

SIEGRUNE.
So, we must be
Dragg'd to thy doom?

BRÜNNHILDE.
Rossweise, sister,
Lend thou me thy courser!

ROSSWEISE.
From Wotan, I trow,
My horse has ne'er fled.

BRÜNNHILDE.
Helmwige, hear me!

HELMWIGE.
My father I follow.

BRÜNNHILDE.
Grimgerde! Gerhilde!
Grant me a steed!
Schwertleite! Siegrune!
See my despair!
O true be ye,
As I aye was true:
Help me this woman to save!

SIEGLINDE.
(Who till now has stared hopelessly into space, starts
up as BRÜNNHILDE puts her arm about her protect-
ingly.)
Nay, sorrow not, strive not for me;
Death alone would I seek!
Who bade thee, maid,
Avert the god's vengeance?
The storm that thunder'd
Had seen me slain
With the self-same weapon
That Siegmund slew:
The end had found me
At peace with him!
Far from Siegmund—
Siegmund, from thee!
O would I were dead,
'Twere less dreadful!—
Lest I should curse
Thee, maid, for thy coming,
Do thou hear me, humbly I pray thee—
Bury thy blade in my heart!

BRÜNNHILDE.
Woman, live on,
For the love of loving!
Rescue the pledge
That his love to thee gave:
A Wälsung soon thou shalt bear!

SIEGLINDE.
(After a moment of alarm, her face beams with joy.)
Rescue me, maiden!
Rescue my child!
Save me, ye maidens,
So mighty to shield!
(Terrible thunderclaps are heard in the distance. They
grow louder.)

WALTRAUTE.
(From the height.)
The storm grows apace!

ORTLINDE.
(As above.)
Flee, ye who fear it!

THE WALKYRS.
Hence with the woman—
Peril she bodes!
No Walkyr would dare
To serve as her shield!

SIEGLINDE
(auf den Knieen vor BRUENNHILDE).

Rette mich, Maid!
Rette die Mutter!

BRUENNHILDE.
(mit schnellem Entschluss).

So fliehe denn eilig —
und fliehe allein!
Ich — bleibe zurück,
biete mich Wotan's Rache:
an mir zögr' ich
den Zürnenden hier,
während du seinem Rasen entrinnst.

SIEGLINDE.

Wohin soll ich mich wenden?

BRUENNHILDE.

Wer von euch, Schwestern,
schweifte nach Osten?

SIEGRUNE.

Nach Osten weithin
dehnt sich ein Wald:
der Niblungen Hort
entführte Fafner dorthin.

SCHWERTLEITE.

Wurmes-Gestalt
schuf sich der Wilde:
in einer Höhle
hütet er Alberich's Reif.

GRIMGERDE.

Nicht geheu'r ist's dort
für ein hülflos Weib.

BRUENNHILDE.

Und doch vor Wotan's Wuth
schützt sie sicher der Wald:
ihn scheut der Mächt'ge
und meidet den Ort.

WALTRAUTE
(von der Höhe).

Furchtbar fährt
dort Wotan zum Fels.

DIE WALKUEREN.

Brünnhilde, hör'
seines Nahens Gebraus'!

BRUENNHILDE
(SIEGLINDEN die Richtung weisend).

Fort denn, eile
nach Osten gewandt!
Muthigen Trotzes
ertrag' alle Müh'n —
Hunger und Durst,
Dorn und Gestein;
lache, ob Noth,
ob Leiden dich nagt!

Denn eines wiss'
und wahr' es immer:
den hehrsten Helden der Welt
hegst du, o Weib,
im schirmenden Schooss! —
(Sie reicht ihr die Stücke von SIEGMUND'S
Schwert.)

Verwahr' ihm die starken
Schwertes-Stücken;
seines Vaters Walstatt
entführt' ich sie glücklich:
der neu gefügt
das Schwert einst schwingt,
den Namen nehm' er von mir —
„Siegfried" erfreu' sich des Sieg's!

SIEGLINDE.

Du hehrstes Wunder!
herrliche Maid!
Dir, Treuen, dank' ich
heiligen Trost!
Für ihn, den wir liebten,
rett' ich das Liebste:
meines Dankes Lohn
lache dir einst!
Lebe wohl!
Dich segnet Sieglinde's Weh'!
(Sie eilt rechts im Vordergrunde ab. —Die Felsen
höhe ist von schwarzen Gewitterwolken umlagert;
furchtbarer Sturm braust aus dem Hintergrunde daher: ein feuriger Schein erhellt den Tannenwald zur
Seite. Zwischen dem Donner hört man WOTAN'S
Ruf.)

WOTAN'S
(Stimme).

Steh'! Brünnhild'!

DIE WALKUEREN.

Den Fels erreichten
Ross und Reiter:
weh', Brünnhild'!
Rache entbrennt!

BRUENNHILDE.

Ach, Schwestern, helft!
mir schwankt das Herz!
Sein Zorn zerschellt mich,
wenn eu'r Schutz ihn nicht zähmt.

DIE WALKUEREN.

Hieher, Verlor'ne!
lass' dich nicht seh'n!
Schmiege dich an uns,
und schweige dem Ruf!
(Sie ziehen sich alle die Felsspitze hinauf, indem sie
BRUENNHIDE unter sich verbergen.)

Weh'!
Wüthend schwingt sich
Wotan vom Ross —
hieher ras't
sein rächender Schritt!
(WOTAN schreitet in furchtbar zürnender Auf-
regung aus dem Tann heraus, und hält vor dem
Haufen der Walküren an, die auf der Höhe eine
Stellung einnehmen, durch welche sie BRUENN-
HILDE schützen.)

SIEGLINDE.
(Kneeling to BRÜNNHILDE.)
Rescue me, maid!
Rescue the mother!

BRÜNNHILDE.
(Coming to a decision quickly.)
Then flee thou, swiftly,
And flee thou alone!
I—here will remain,
Waiting for Wotan's vengeance:
On me falleth
His furious ire,
And his wrath thou meanwhile shalt
escape.

SIEGLINDE.
Where, ah where shall I wander?

BRÜNNHILDE.
Which of ye sisters
Speedeth to eastward?

SIEGRUNE.
A wood there lies
Far hence, in the East:
The Nibelung's hoard
By Fafner hath there been hid.

SCHWERTLEITE.
Shaped as a worm,
Fafner lies lurking
In a deep cavern
Watching o'er Alberich's ring.

GRIMGERDE.
'Tis a dreadful spot
For a helpless wife!

BRÜNNHILDE.
And yet from Wotan's wrath
Safe were she in the wood:
For, though so mighty,
The forest he shuns.

WALTRAUTE.
(From the height.)
Wildly now
Rides Wotan our way!

THE WALKYRS.
Brünnhilde, hear
The loud roar as he nears!

BRÜNNHILDE.
(Directing SIEGLINDE.)
Hence then, hasten
And hide in the East!
Bravely and boldly
Enduring thy woe—
Hunger and thirst,
Hardship and pain;
Laugh, altho' need
And sorrow should gnaw!

For one thing e'er
Hold fast and treasure:
The noblest hero on earth
Soon from thy womb
Shall leap into life!
(She hands her the fragments of SIEGMUND's sword.)
The sword that was shiver'd,
See thou save him:
From his father's death-field
I brought the bits safely:
Who, newly forged,
The sword shall swing,
The name I give him shall bear—
"Siegfried," a Victor shall stand!

SIEGLINDE.
Thou glorious wonder!
Valorous maid!
Thy truth has lent me
Courage and trust!
For him, whom we honored,
Save I my dearest:
Would that thanks alone
Thee could repay!
Fare thee well!
Be blest by Sieglinde's woe!
(She hurries away on the right.—The summit of the
rocks is enveloped in dark thunderclouds. A terrible
storm grows in the background. A lurid glow appears
in the fir-trees. Between the thunderclaps WOTAN's
voice is heard.)

WOTAN'S VOICE.
Stay, Brünnhild'!

THE WALKYRS.
The steed and rider
Rush to reach us:
Woe, Brünnhild'!
Wild is his wrath!

BRÜNNHILDE.
Ah, sisters, help!
My heart grows faint!
Unless ye tame him
I am undone now, and doomed!

THE WALKYRS.
Hide here, o lost one,
Lest thou be seen!
Cling thou close to us
And heed not his call!
(All ascend to the top of the peak, concealing BRÜNN-
HILDE.)
Woe!
Wildly Wotan
Leaps from his steed—
See how fierce
He flames on his way!
(WOTAN, frenzied with anger, issues from the firs
and halts at the foot of the height on which the
WALKYRS are grouped, hiding BRÜNNHILDE.)

WOTAN.

Wo ist Brünnhild'?
Wo die Verbrecherin?
Wagt ihr, die Böse
vor mir zu bergen?

DIE WALKUEREN.

Schrecklich ertos't dein Toben: —
was thaten, Vater, die Töchter,
dass sie dich reizten
zu rasender Wuth?

WOTAN.

Wollt ihr mich höhnen?
Hütet euch, Freche!
Ich weiss: Brünnhilde
bergt ihr vor mir.
Weichet von ihr,
der ewig Verworf'nen,
wie ihren Werth
von sich sie warf!

DIE WALKUEREN.

Zu uns floh die Verfolgte,
uns'ren Schutz flehte sie an!
mit Furcht und Zagen
fasst sie dein Zorn.
Für die bange Schwester
bitten wir nun,
dass den ersten Zorn du bezähm'st.

WOTAN.

Weichherziges
Weibergezücht!
So matten Muth
gewannt ihr von mir?
Erzog ich euch kühn,
zu Kämpfen zu zieh'n,
schuf ich die Herzen
euch hart und scharf,
dass ihr Wilden nun weint und greint,
wenn mein Grimm eine Treulose straft?
So wisst denn, Winselnde,
was die verbrach,
um die euch Zagen
die Zähre entbrennt!
Keine wie sie
kannte mein innerstes Sinnen!
keine wie sie
wusste den Quell meines Willens;
sie selbst war
meines Wunsches schaffender Schooss:
und so nun brach sie
den seligen Bund,
dass treulos sie
meinem Willen getrotzt,
mein herrschend Gebot
offen verhöhnt,
gegen mich die Waffe gewandt,
die allein mein Wunsch ihr schuf! —

Hörst du's, Brünnhilde?
du, der ich Brünne,
Helm und Wehr,
Wonne und Huld,
Namen und Leben verlieh?
Hörst du mich Klage erheben,
und birgst dich bang dem Kläger,
dass feig' du der Straf' entflöh'st?

BRUENNHILDE

(tritt aus der Schaar der W a l k ü r e n hervor, schrei
tet demüthigen, doch festen Schrittes von der Felsen
spitze herab und tritt so in geringer Ferne vo
WOTAN).

Hier bin ich, Vater:
gebiete die Strafe!

WOTAN.

Nicht — straf' ich dich erst:
deine Strafe schufst du dir selbst.
Durch meinen Willen
warst du allein:
gegen mich doch hast du gewollt;
meine Befehle nur
führtest du aus:
gegen mich doch hast du befohlen;
Wunsch-Maid
war'st du mir:
gegen mich doch hast du gewünscht;
Schild-Maid
war'st du mir:
gegen mich doch hob'st du den Schild;
Loos-Kieserin
war'st du mir:
gegen mich doch kies'test du Loose;
Helden-Reizerin
war'st du mir:
gegen mich doch reiztest du Helden.
Was sonst du war'st,
sagte dir Wotan:
was jetzt du bist,
das sage dir selbst!
Wunschmaid bist du nicht mehr;
Walküre bist du gewesen: —
nun sei fortan,
was so du noch bist!

BRUENNHILDE

(heftig erschrocken).

Du verstössest mich?
versteh' ich den Sinn?

WOTAN.

Nicht send' ich dich mehr aus Walhall,
nicht weis' ich dir mehr
Helden zur Wal;
nicht führ'st du mehr Sieger
in meinen Saal:
bei der Götter trautem Mahle
das Trinkhorn nicht reichst du
traulich mir mehr;
nicht kos' ich dir mehr

WOTAN.
Where is Brünnhild'?
She who betrayeth me?
Dare ye the guilty
From me to shelter?

THE WALKYRS.
Fearful thy fury rages:—
What did thy daughters, o father,
Thus to awaken
Thine anger and rage?

WOTAN.
Would ye then mock me?
Dare ye defy me?
I know: Brünnhilde
Fain would ye hide.
Shrink from her, ay,
Forsake her, the traitress,
For she her *self*
Hath now betrayed!

THE WALKYRS.
To us fled she, thy victim;
She implored, wept for our aid!
Now worn and woeful
Dreads she thy wrath!
We entreat thee, father,
Pity thy child!
Let her sorrow soften thy heart!

WOTAN.
Weak-hearted and
Womanly brood!
So faint and slow
Ye fancy your sire?
For this were ye taught
To battle and war,
Hardened and heartened
To dare and do?
Would ye weep and whimper and groan
When my wrath on the criminal falls?
Then wist ye, whimperers,
What is the crime
Of her who draws
From your terror these tears?
None of ye all
Knew as she knew what I purposed.
None of ye all
Fathomed my will and my meaning;
Herself was
She the soul and source of my will:
And *she* has broken
Our holiest bond,
For faithless what
I had willed she defied,
My solemn behest
Openly braved—
Against me the weapons she turned
That my will alone had wrought!—

Hear'st thou, Brünnhilde?
Thou to whom buckler,
Helm and spear,
Being and honor I lent?
Hearest thou how I accuse thee,
And dost thou hide and tremble
In dread of the doom thou'dst fled?

BRÜNNHILDE.
(Issues from the group formed by the other WALKYRS,
descends humbly, but with a firm step, from the peak,
and halts at a little distance from WOTAN.)
Here am I, father:
My doom do thou order!

WOTAN.
Nay—*I* do not doom:
By thy deed thyself thou hast doomed.
My will, mine only,
Gave thee thy life:
Yet against that will thou hast warred.
Naught but my bidding
Thou once didst obey:
Yet against me now thou hast bidden;
Wish-maid
Wast thou once:
Yet against me now thou hast willed;
Shield-maid
Wast thou once:
Yet against me raisest thy shield;
Fate-messenger
Wast thou once:
Yet against me fate thou wast moving;
Hero-ravisher
Wast thou once:
Yet against me turnest thou heroes.
What more thou wast
Wotan hath told thee:
What now thou art,
Thyself should best know!
Wish-maid art thou no more;
Walkyrie art thou no longer:—
Henceforth then be
What only thou canst!

BRÜNNHILDE.
(In terrible agitation.)
Thou wouldst cast me out?
Is that thy decree?

WOTAN.
No more thou'lt ride now from Walhall;
No more shalt thou bid
Heroes to death;
No more bring the victors
To fill my hall:
When together gods are gathered
My horn thou shalt never
Bring me to drain;
No more I can kiss

den kindischen Mund.
Von göttlicher Schaar
bist du geschieden,
ausgestossen
aus der Ewigen Stamm;
gebrochen ist unser Bund:
aus meinem Angesicht bist du verbannt.

DIE WALKUEREN.
(in Jammer ausbrechend).

Wehe! Weh'!
Schwester! Ach Schwester!

BRUENNHILDE.
Nimmst du mir alles,
was einst du gab'st?

WOTAN.
Der dich zwingt, wird dir's entzieh'n!
Hieher auf den Berg
banne ich dich;
in wehrlosen Schlaf
schliess' ich dich fest;
der Mann dann fange die Maid,
der am Wege sie findet und weckt.

DIE WALKUEREN.
Halt', o Vater!
halt' ein den Fluch!
Soll die Maid verblüh'n
und verbleichen dem Mann?
Ach, wende von ihr
die schreiende Schmach,
schrecklicher Gott!
wie die Schwester, träf' uns der Schimpf!

WOTAN.
Hörtet ihr nicht,
was ich verhängt?
Aus eurer Schaar
ist die treulose Schwester geschieden;
mit euch zu Ross
durch die Lüfte nicht reitet sie länger;
die magdliche Blume
verblüht der Maid;
ein Gatte gewinnt
ihre weibliche Gunst:
dem herrischen Manne
gehorcht sie fortan,
am Herde sitzt sie und spinnt,
aller Spottenden Ziel und Spiel.
(BRUENNHILDE sinkt schreiend vor seinen Füssen
zu Boden; die W a l k ü r e n machen eine Bewegung
des Entsetzens.)
Schreckt euch ihr Loos?
So flieht die Verlor'ne!
Weichet von ihr
und haltet euch fern!
Wer von euch wagte
bei ihr zu weilen,

wer mir zum Trotz
zu der Traurigen hielt',
die Thörin theilte ihr Loos:
das künd' ich der Kühnen an! —
Fort jetzt von hier!
meidet den Felsen!
Hurtig jagt mir von hinnen,
sonst erharrt Jammer euch hier!

DIE WALKUEREN.
Weh'! Weh'!
(Die W a l k ü r e n fahren mit wildem Wehschrei
auseinander und stürzen in hastiger Flucht in den
Tann: bald hört man sie wie mit Sturm auf ihren
Rossen davonjagend. — Nach und nach legt sich
während des Folgenden das Gewitter; die Wolken
verziehen sich: Abenddämmerung, und endlich Nacht,
sinken bei ruhigem Wetter herein.
WOTAN und BRUENNHILDE, die noch zu seinen
Füssen hingestreckt liegt, sind allein zurückgeblieben.
— Langes, feierliches Schweigen: unveränderte Stel
lung WOTAN'S und BRUENNHILDE'S.

BRUENNHILDE
(endlich das Haupt langsam erhebend, sucht WO-
TAN'S noch abgewandten Blick und richtet sich während des Folgenden allmälig ganz auf).

War es so schmählich,
was ich verbrach,
dass mein Verbrechen so schmählich du
bestraf'st?
War es so niedrig,
was ich dir that,
dass du so tief mir Erniedrigung
schaff'st?
War es so ehrlos,
was ich beging,
dass mein Vergeh'n nun die Ehre mir
raubt?
O sag', Vater,
sieh' mir in's Auge:
schweige den Zorn,
zähme die Wuth!
Deute mir hell
Die dunkle Schuld,
die mit starrem Trotze dich zwingt,
zu verstossen dein trautestes Kind!

WOTAN
(finster).

Frag' deine That —
sie deutet dir deine Schuld!

BRUENNHILDE.
Deinen Befehl
führte ich aus.

WOTAN.
Befahl ich dir
für den Wälsung zu fechten?

BRUENNHILDE.
So hiessest du mich
als Herrscher der Wal.

WOTAN.
Doch meine Weisung
nahm ich wieder zurück.

Thine innocent lips.
The gods thou didst meet
Know thee no longer;
Outcast art thou
From the race of the gods.
For broken now is our bond,
nd from my presence thou'rt banished
for aye!

THE WALKYRS.
(Lamenting.)
Woe, ah, woe!
Ah, sister, o sister!

BRÜNNHILDE.
All thou art taking
That once thou gav'st?

WOTAN.
He, thy lord—takes it away!
Now here to this hill
Banish I thee;
Unguarded to sleep
Sentence I thee;
'hat man shall capture the maid,
Vho shall wake her to life on his way.

THE WALKYRS.
Have done! O father,
Enough thou'st cursed!
Must the maiden pale
And be prey to a man?
O turn from her head
This terrible shame,
Merciless god!
Dr our sister's woe and her fate let us
share!

WOTAN.
Did ye not hear
What I decreed?
Far from you all
hall your renegade sister be driven;
With ye no more
'hrough the air she shall ride on her
charger;
Her maidenly blossom
Shall fail and fade;
A husband shall win her
And wear her for wife;
A man and a master
Shall hold her in thrall,
At home she'll sit and she'll spin,
As a mock and a mark for scorn.
Brünnhilde shrieks and falls at his feet. The Wal-
kyrs are convulsed with terror.)
Fear ye her fate?
Then flee from the outcast.
Leave her to bear
Her sentence alone!
She who would venture
Near her to linger,

She who should venture
Her crime to condone,
Shall surely share in her doom:
I warn ye, so hear and heed!—
Up and begone!
Haunt not the mountain!
Haste ye hence, as I bid ye,
Lest ye all rue your delay!

THE WALKYRS.
Woe! Woe!
(The Walkyrs disperse, with wild lamentations, and
rush away into the fir-trees. Shortly after they are
heard riding away at a furious gallop. The storm
gradually abates. The clouds clear off, dusk comes
and then at last is merged into placid night.)
(Wotan remains alone with Brünnhilde, who is still
prostrate at his feet. A long, solemn silence follows,
during which Wotan and Brünnhilde do not stir.)

BRÜNNHILDE.
(Slowly lifts her head, seeking response from Wo-
tan's averted eyes. Then she rises.)
Was it so shameful,
All I have done,
That my misdoings should steep me so
in shame?
Sinned I so deeply,
When I did sin,
That thou should'st sink me so deep in
disgrace?
Had I no honor,
E'en in my guilt,
That thou of honor must rob me for aye?
Ah, speak, father,
Face me now frankly:
Silence thy wrath,
Stifle thy rage!
And tell me, I pray,
My deadly crime,
That compels thee ruthless to be,
And an outcast to make of thy child!

WOTAN.
(Gloomily.)
Question thy crime—
'Twill show the depth of thy guilt!

BRÜNNHILDE.
Thine own behest
'Twas I obey'd.

WOTAN.
And did I bid
Thee to fight for the Wälsung?

BRÜNNHILDE.
So didst thou command
As master of war.

WOTAN.
Ay, but my bidding
Swiftly did I revoke.

BRUENNHILDE.
Als Fricka den eig'nen
Sinn dir entfremdet:
da ihrem Sinn du dich fügtest,
warst du selber dir Feind.

WOTAN
(bitter).
Dass du mich verstanden, wähnt' ich,
und strafte den wissenden Trotz;
doch feig' und dumm
dachtest du mich:
so hätt' ich Verrath nicht zu rächen,
zu gering wär'st du meinem Grimm?

BRUENNHILDE.
Nicht weise bin ich;
doch wusst' ich das Eine —
dass den Wälsung du liebtest:
ich wusste den Zwiespalt,
der dich zwang,
dies Eine ganz zu vergessen.
Das And're musstest
einzig du seh'n,
was zu schau'n so herb
schmerzte dein Herz —
dass Siegmund Schutz du versagtest.

WOTAN.
Du wusstest es so,
und wagtest dennoch den Schutz?

BRUENNHILDE.
Weil für dich im Auge
das Eine ich hielt,
dem, im Zwange des And'ren
schmerzlich entzweit,
rathlos den Rücken du wandtest.
Die im Kampfe Wotan
den Rücken bewacht,
die sah nun das nur,
was du nicht sah'st: —
Siegmund musst' ich seh'n.
Tod kündend
trat ich vor ihn,
gewahrte sein Auge,
hörte sein Wort;
ich vernahm des Helden
heilige Noth;
tönend erklang mir
des Tapfersten Klage —
freiester Liebe
furchtbares Leid,
traurigsten Muthes
mächtigster Trotz:
meinem Ohr' erscholl,
mein Aug' erschaute,
was tief im Busen das Herz
zu heil'gem Beben mir traf. —
Scheu und staunend
stand ich in Scham:

ihm nur zu dienen
konnt' ich noch denken:
Sieg oder Tod
mit Siegmund zu theilen —
diess nur erkannt' ich
zu kiesen als Loos!
Der diese Liebe
mir in's Herz gehaucht,
dem Willen, der
dem Wälsung mich gesellt,
ihm innig vertraut —
trotzt' ich deinem Gebot.

WOTAN.
So thatest du,
was so gern zu thun ich begeh, —
doch was nicht zu thun
die Noth zwiefach mich zwang?
So leicht wähntest du
Wonne des Herzes erworben,
wo brennend Weh'
in das Herz mir brach,
wo grässliche Noth
den Grimm mir schuf,
einer Welt zu Liebe
der Liebe Quell
im gequälten Herzen zu hemmen?
Wo gegen mich selber
ich sehrend mich wandte,
aus Ohnmacht-Schmerzen
schäumend ich aufschoss,
wüthender Sehnsucht
sengender Wunsch
den schrecklichen Willen mir schuf,
in den Trümmern der eig'nen Welt
meine ew'ge Trauer zu enden: —
da labte süss
dich, selige Lust;
wonniger Rührung
üppigen Rausch
enttrankst du lachend
der Liebe Trank —
als mir göttlicher Noth
nagende Galle gemischt?
Deinen leichten Sinn
lass' dich denn leiten:
von mir sagtest du dich los!
Dich muss ich meiden,
gemeinsam mit dir
nicht darf ich Rath mehr raunen;
getrennt nicht dürfen
traut wir mehr schaffen:
so weit Leben und Luft,
darf der Gott dir nicht mehr begegnen.

BRUENNHILDE.
Wohl taugte dir nicht
die thör'ge Maid,
die staunend im Rathe
nicht dich verstand

BRÜNNHILDE.

When Fricka thine honest
Mind had perverted:
By giving way to content her,
Thou thyself didst betray.

WOTAN.
(Bitterly.)

Thou didst understand me, clearly:
Thy wilful rebellion I scourge.
But weak and dull
Seemed I to thee:
Should treason itself go unpunished,
Too unworthy wert thou for wrath?

BRÜNNHILDE.

No wisdom have I
Yet this I knew surely—
That thou lovedst the Wälsung.
I knew of the quarrel
That compelled
Thy heart to seem so forgetful.
No help was left thee
But to behold
What with shame and pain
So harrowed up thy heart —
And Siegmund soon was forsaken.

WOTAN.

Thou knewest it well,
And yet thou didst stand his shield?

BRÜNNHILDE.

Ay, for *thee,* thee only,
I did not forget,
When, a thrall to another,
Sad and alone,
Helpless away thou didst turn thee.
She who Wotan's rearguard
In battle had been
Could see what thou
Now no more couldst see:
Siegmund straight I sought.
Death-dooming,
Went I my way,
And, meeting his glances,
Heard what he spake;
Then I knew the hero's
Terrible woe;
Thrilled as I sounded
His valor and sorrow—
Heard him unbosom
Anguish and love,
Sad and yet dauntless,
Daring and strong:
What mine ear did hear,
And eye did fathom,
Awoke and tortured my heart
With holy passion and pain.
Awed, astounded,
Stood I in shame:

Now thinking only
How I could serve him:
Triumph or death
With Siegmund beside me—
This could I only
Of fortune demand!
Him who this love
Within my heart had roused,
The will that had the Wälsung
To me bound,
In faith and in trust—
Dared I now to defy.

WOTAN.

So *thou* didst do
What I once indeed had desired—
But what not to do
By fate fast I was bound?
So soon hopedst thou
Rapture would pay thee for loving,
When burning woe
In my heart did flame,
And terrible need
My wrath compelled,
For the sake of saving
A world with love,
In my heart to dry up love's sources?
When, turning against
My own self all my anger,
In helpless sorrow
Fiercely I struggled,
Passionate longing
Raging awoke,
The merciless wish in me roused,
In the wreck of the world I ruled
My unending sorrow to bury:—
And thou didst dream
Of joy and of love,
Revel in rapture,
Riot in bliss;
Didst drain, delighted,
The draught of love—
While I, god though I be,
Poisoned my bosom with gall?
Let thy wanton will
Lead thee hereafter:
From me now thyself thou'st loosed!
Now are we severed;
Together with thee
No more I'll come for counsel·
We twain can never
Plan to work wonders:
So, while life shall be thine,
From the god thou'rt parted for ever!

BRÜNNHILDE.

As naught thou dost hold
The foolish maid
Who, seeking thy meaning,
Misunderstood;

wie mein eig'ner Rath
nur das Eine mir rieth —
zu lieben, was du geliebt. —
Muss ich denn scheiden
und scheu dich meiden,
musst du spalten,
was einst sich umspannt,
die eig'ne Hälfte
fern' von dir halten —
dass sonst sie ganz dir gehörte,
du, Gott, vergiss das nicht!
Dein ewig Theil
nicht wirst du entehren,
Schande nicht wollen,
die dich beschimpft;
dich selbst liessest du sinken,
säh'st du dem Spott mich zum Spiel!

WOTAN.

Du folgtest selig
der Liebe Macht:
folge nun dem,
den du lieben musst!

BRUENNHILDE.

Soll ich aus Walhall scheiden,
nicht mehr mit dir schaffen und walten:
dem herrischen Manne
gehorchen fortan —
dem feigen Prahler
gieb mich nicht Preis!
nicht werthlos sei er,
der mich gewinnt.

WOTAN.

Von Walvater schiedest du —
nicht wählen darf er für dich.

BRUENNHILDE.

Du zeugtest ein edles Geschlecht;
kein Zager kann je ihm entschlagen:
der weiblichste Held — ich weiss es —
entblüht dem Wälsungenstamm.

WOTAN.

Schweig' von dem Wälsungenstamm!
von dir geschieden
schied ich von ihm:
vernichten musst' ihn der Neid.

BRUENNHILDE.

Die von dir sich riss —
rettete ihn:
Sieglinde hegt
die heiligste Frucht;
in Schmerz und Leid,
wie kein Weib sie gelitten,
wird sie gebären,
was bang sie birgt .

WOTAN.

Nie suche bei mir
Schutz für die Frau,
noch für ihres Schoosses Frucht!

BRUENNHILDE.

Sie wahret das Schwert,
das du Siegmund schufest. —

WOTAN.

Und das ich ihm in Stücken schlug
Nicht streb', o Maid,
den Muth mir zu stören!
Erwarte dein Loos,
wie sich's dir wirft:
nicht kiesen kann ich es dir! —
Doch fort muss ich jetzt,
fern mich verzieh'n:
zuviel schon zögert' ich hier.
Von der Abwendigen
wend' ich mich ab;
nicht wissen darf ich,
was sie sich wünscht:
die Strafe nur
muss vollstreckt ich seh'n.

BRUENNHILDE.

Was hast du erdacht,
dass ich erdulde?

WOTAN

In festen Schlaf
verschliess' ich dich:
wer so die Wehrlose weckt,
dem ward, erwacht, sie zum Weib.

BRUENNHILDE
(stürzt auf ihre Kniee).

Soll fesselnder Schlaf
fest mich binden,
dem feigsten Manne
zur leichten Beute:
diess Eine musst du erhören,
was heil'ge Angst zu dir fleht!
Die Schlafende schütze
mit scheuchenden Schrecken:
dass nur ein furchtlos
freiester Held
hier auf dem Felsen
einst mich fänd'!

WOTAN.

Zu viel begehrst du —
zu viel der Gunst!

BRUENNHILDE
(seine Kniee umfassend).

Dies Eine musst —
du erhören!
Zerknicke dein Kind,

To her simple mind
One thing only was meant—
To love what thy heart had loved.—
Must we be parted
For aye, and sundered?
Must thou sever
What once was entwined?
Ah, wouldst thou banish
Half of thy being—
Who long obeyed thee so blindly,
Thou god, forget not that!
Thy deathless self
Thou wilt not dishonor,
Couldst not repay me
With shame for shame;
Thyself wouldst thou but punish,
Wert thou to mock me with scorn!

WOTAN.
Thou'st yielded lightly
Where love allured.
Yield thyself now
To a love foredoomed!

BRÜNNHILDE.
Must I then leave Walhalla—
No more with thee reign and do battle?
Bow down and be mastered
At beck of a man?
Then give no braggart
Boaster the prize!
Let no worthless coward
Thy daughter win!

WOTAN.
The War-Father thou'st disowned—
He may not choose thee the man.

BRÜNNHILDE.
A valorous race thou'st begot;
No coward could come of thy breeding:
A hero alone—that know I—
Of Wälsung blood could be born.

WOTAN.
Leave thou the Wälsungs in peace!
From them I parted,
Parting with thee:
Twas envy doomed them to die.

BRÜNNHILDE.
She who's rent from thee
Rescued their race:
Sieglinde bears
The holiest fruit;
In pain and woe
Such as none have e'er suffered,
What in her's hidden
To life she brings.

WOTAN.
Yet hope not from me
Help for her pain,
Nor for her unhallow'd child!

BRÜNNHILDE.
The sword she has saved
Thou to Siegmund sentest.

WOTAN.
And that I into splinters split!
Seek not, o maid,
My mind to unsettle!
Await thou the lot
Thy sin has earned:
I may not change it for thee.
And now I must hence:
Far from this place.
Too long I've lingered to-day.
Now I turn from thee
As thou didst from me;
Forbidden am I
Thy wish to learn:
Thy crime alone
I must see punished.

BRÜNNHILDE.
What hast thou conceived
That I must suffer?

WOTAN.
In slumber deep
Thine eyes I lock:
He who the sleeper awakes
Shall win, and wear, her for wife.

BRÜNNHILDE.
(Falling on her knees.)
Lest fettering sleep
Fast should bind me
The prey and booty
Of any coward:
One boon thou wilt not deny me
As deep in anguish I pray!
The sleeper, o, shelter
With ramparts of terror.
A hero only,
Fearless and free,
Here to the mountain
Then could come!

WOTAN.
Too much thou askest—
Too great's the grace!

BRÜNNHILDE.
(Clinging to his knees.)
This boon thou must—
Not deny me!
Ah, crush out the life

das dein Knie umfasst;
zertritt die Traute,
zertrümm're die Maid;
ihres Leibes Spur
zerstöre dein Speer:
doch gieb, Grausamer, nicht
der grässlichsten Schmach sie preis!
(Mit Wildheit.)
Auf dein Gebot
entbrenne ein Feuer;
den Felsen umglühe
lodernde Gluth:
es leck' ihre Zung',
es fresse ihr Zahn
den Zagen, der frech sich wagte,
dem freislichen Felsen zu nah'n!

WOTAN
(blickt ihr ergriffen in das Auge und hebt sie auf).
Leb' wohl, du kühnes,
herrliches Kind!
Du meines Herzens
heiligster Stolz,
leb' wohl! leb' wohl! leb' wohl!
Muss ich dich meiden,
und darf nicht minnig
mein Gruss dich mehr grüssen;
sollst du nun nicht mehr
neben mir reiten,
noch Meth beim Mahl mir reichen,
muss ich verlieren
dich, die ich liebe,
du lachende Lust meines Auges: —
ein bräutliches Feuer
soll dir nun brennen,
wie nie einer Braut es gebrannt!
Flammende Gluth
umglühe den Fels;
mit zehrenden Schrecken
scheuch' es den Zagen,
der Feige fliehe
Brünnhilde's Fels: —
denn Einer nur freie die Braut,
der freier als ich, der Gott!
(BRUENNHILDE wirft sich ihm gerührt und entzückt in die Arme.)
Der Augen leuchtendes Paar,
das oft ich lächelnd gekos't,
wenn Kampfes-Lust

ein Kuss dir lohnte,
wenn kindisch lallend
der Helden Lob
von holden Lippen dir floss: —
dieser Augen strahlendes Paar,
das oft im Sturm mir geglänzt,
wenn Hoffnungs-Sehnen
das Herz mir sengte,
nach Welten-Wonne
mein Wunsch verlangte
aus wild webendem Bangen: —
zum letzten Mal
letz' es mich heut'
mit des Lebewohles
letztem Kuss!
Dem glücklicher'n Manne
glänze sein Stern;
dem unseligen Ew'gen
muss es scheidend sich schliessen!
Denn so — kehrt
der Gott sich dir ab:
so küsst er die Gottheit von dir.
(Er küsst sie auf beide Augen, die ihr sogleich ve
schlossen bleiben: sie sinkt sanft ermattend in seine
Armen zurück. Er geleitet sie zart auf einen niedrige
Mooshügel zu liegen, über den sich eine breitästig
Tanne ausstreckt. Noch einmal betrachtet er ih
Züge und schliesst ihr dann den Helm fest zu; dan
verweilt sein Blick nochmals schmerzlich auf ihre
Gestalt, die er endlich mit dem langen Stahlschil
der Walküre zudeckt. — Dann schreitet er m
feierlichen Entschlusse in die Mitte der Bühne u
kehrt die Spitze seines Speeres gegen einen mächtig
Felsstein.)
Loge hör'!
lausche hieher!
Wie zuerst ich dich fand
als feurige Gluth,
wie dann einst du mir schwandest
als schweifende Lohe:
wie ich dich band,
bann' ich dich heut'!
Herauf, wabernde Lohe,
umlod're mir feurig den Fels!
Loge! Loge! Hieher!
(Bei der letzten Anrufung schlägt er mit der Sp
des Speeres dreimal auf den Stein, worauf diesem
Feuerstrahl entfährt, der schnell zu einem Flammen
meere anschwillt, dem WOTAN mit einem Wink
seiner Speerspitze den Umkreis des Felsens als Strö
mung zuweist.)
Wer meines Speeres
Spitze fürchtet,
durchschreite das Feuer nie!
(Er verschwindet in der Gluth nach dem Hinter
grunde zu. — Der Vorhang fällt.)

DAS ENDE.

Of thy child who kneels;
Destroy thy servant,
The truest of maids;
With thy mighty lance
Her bosom transpierce;
But give, gruesome one, not
Thy daughter to scorn and shame!
(Wildly.)
At thy command
Let threatening fires
The mountain encircle,
Raven and glow:
And, heavenward leaping,
Pitiless tongues
Strike terror in him who'd venture
The desolate rock to invade!

WOTAN.

Gazes with emotion into her eyes, and helps her to rise.)

Farewell, thou bravest,
Rarest of maids!
Thou, my heart's treasure,
Idol and pride,
Farewell! farewell! farewell!
Must I forsake thee
And now may never
My soul send thee greeting:
Shalt thou no more, then,
Near me go riding,
Nor bring me mead to cheer me;
Must I then lose thee,
O, my belovèd,
Thou laughter and light in my sorrow:—
For thee will I kindle
Burning red beacons
That never for bride had yet flamed!
Ruddy the fire
Shall glow round the rock;
With raging and roaring
Taunting the coward;
Who fears shall flee from
Brünnhilde's bed:—
For he alone frees her, the bride,
Who's freer than I, the god!
Overcome with joyous emotion, Brünnhilde throws herself into his arms.)
O, eyes aglow with delight,
That oft I tenderly wooed,
When lust of strife

A kiss had won thee,
When, gently opening,
Thy maiden lips
The heroes' praises would sing;
O, dear eyes that oft in the storm
Would beam and brighten my way,
When hope and passion
My heart set longing
For earthly rapture
And bliss of loving,
With wild wishing and dreading:
A parting kiss
Take ye to-night,
As I bid farewell
To light and bliss!
Your starry-bright glances
Keep for the man;
On me luckless immortal
Ye are closing for ever!
For thus—doth
The god thee renounce:
Thus kissing thy godhead away.
(He kisses both her eyes, which at once close. She sinks insensible in his arms. He bears her tenderly to a low mossy bank, shaded by the wide-spreading branches of a great fir-tree. Once more he gazes on her features. Then he closes her helmet tightly. Again he looks sorrowfully at her recumbent form, which he at last covers with the Walkyr's steel shield. Then, with solemn determination, he moves to the centre of the stage, and points the head of his spear toward a mighty rock.)
Loge, hear!
Lend me thine ear!
As at first thee I found,
A fiery flame,
As thou erst didst escape me,
A-leaping and glowing:
As thou wast bound,
Bind I thee now:
Arise, flaring and glowing,
Ring round the whole mountain with fire!
Loge! Loge! Arise!
(After the last invocation Wotan strikes the rock three times with the point of his spear, whereupon a flame leaps up. It soon grows into a sea of flames, which, with a motion of his spear, Wotan confines in a circle that hems round the rock.)
Who from my spear-point
Shrinks in terror,
Shall never the flame defy!
(He disappears in the background amid the flames. The curtain falls.)

THE END.

DIE WALKÜRE.

DIE WALKÜRE.

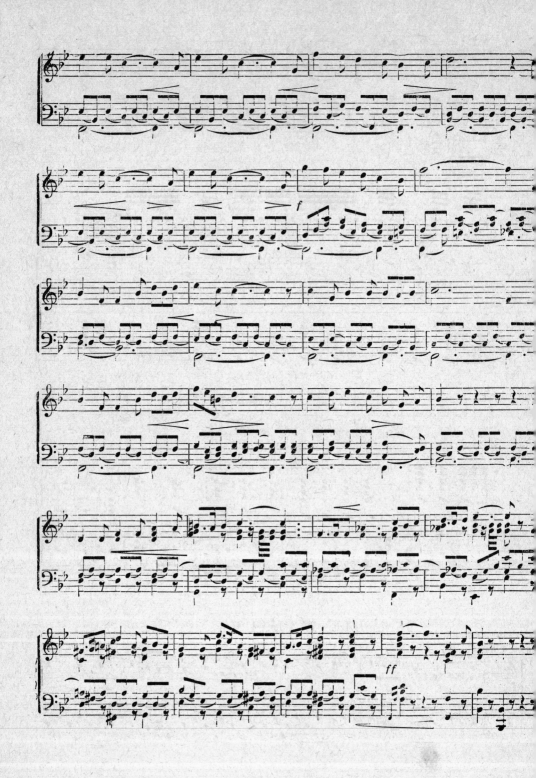